FINDING A GRACE-FILLED LIFE

Rick Mathis, PhD

D1526951

Paulist Press
New York/Mahwah, NJ

Cover design by Joy Taylor
Crosswalk photo © Justin Horrocks; butterfly and collage by Joy Taylor
Book design by Lynn Else

Library of Congress Cataloging-in-Publication Data

Mathis, Rick.
    Finding a grace-filled life / Rick Mathis.
        p. cm.
    Includes bibliographical references.
    ISBN 978-0-8091-4528-7 (alk. paper)
    1. Spiritual life—Christianity. 2. Spirituality. 3. Christian life.
I. Title.
    BV4501.3.M287 2008
    248.4—dc22

                                                      2008013932

Published by Paulist Press
997 Macarthur Boulevard
Mahwah, New Jersey 07430

www.paulistpress.com

Printed and bound in the
United States of America

Contents

Introduction

I deas for books often arise out of unusual experiences. The idea for a book on grace seemed to come out of nowhere and remained on my mind for some time. I kept coming back to the phrase "ready or not" and thinking about how we often go out into the world with the same sort of joy and expectation as when we played games as children. Yet our youthful enthusiasm wanes when we encounter the difficulties associated with the game of life. Our experience of grace can have much the same quality. We may be aware of all sorts of spiritual practices that engender grace, but this experience fades when we face a world filled with deadlines and difficulties. My hope was to build a bridge between these practices and our daily experience to overcome this problem.

During the time that I spent writing and revising this book I have continued to be impressed by the various currents of life and the availability of grace to help us navigate them. Exciting opportunities sometimes leap out at us and make life a wonderful adventure. Then difficulties come up that must be weathered. I meet young people and am reminded of the promise and passion of youth, and then hear about former teachers and mentors dealing with illness or passing away and am reminded of the fragile and transitory nature of our earthly existence.

Yet God's grace remains throughout. It has a way of changing things when I let it, particularly my reaction to what is going on around me. It enables me to be open to the strangers that come along, and to take the good that I have learned from people in my past and to try to pass that along to others through my words and conduct. Most importantly, grace seasons my life, creating the small changes that, with care and attention, can lead to more profound ones. If this book in any way helps you to experience this "graceful" process as well, then it will have achieved its aim.

By way of acknowledgment, I am fortunate in having a number of friends, family, and co-workers who positively influence me both as a person and as a writer. First and foremost is my wife and best friend, Karen, who has stayed with me throughout the many years of our marriage. My children, Lee and Erica, remind me of the energy of youth and keep me from succumbing to my stodgy ways. Joel Huffstetler shares my love for writing and the written word and is a source for many interesting theological and philosophical conversations. Steve Martin (not the comedian) is a friend whom I see as a true moral and spiritual exemplar. Doctor Ken Patric and Dr. Steve Coulter are mentors who have been both kind and supportive over my years at BlueCross BlueShield of Tennessee. Joe Jucewicz is a graduate school buddy who offers many words of encouragement as well as insights into matters political, literary, and spiritual, while Darryl Rowe keeps me focused and reminds me not to take myself too seriously. As far as the text of the book is concerned, my editor at Paulist Press, Kevin DiCamillo, combined some superb editing with a consistently positive and enthusiastic attitude. Such qualities are invaluable to a writer.

CHAPTER ONE
Ready or Not

*E*ach day you have the opportunity to live a new life. This simply means casting off your old ways of thinking and feeling the warmth of God's grace around you. I'm sure that you have experienced this newness and grace in the past. But then something happened and you went back to your old ways of thinking and being.

There are ways of continuing to experience this newness. One way is to work with the spaces that exist in your life. Even the busiest of lives have spaces. These are moments when, if you choose to, you can meditate or simply reflect upon your life. You may have a few insights, reaffirm some beliefs, or set new goals before getting back into the world. Such moments can make a profound difference in your life and even in the world. They also help by simply providing enough of an experience of God's grace to get you through the day.

In some respects such moments can be compared to the time-honored game of hide-and-seek. The person who is "it" leans against a tree or wall, closes his or her eyes, and counts to ten before trying to find the first hidden person. While counting, no doubt, the person is engaged in devising some strategy, thinking about where to look first. Then it's time to turn and face the task at hand, usually by shouting a hearty "ready or not, here I come."

Spiritual practices are in some respects similar to hide-and-seek. We may pray or meditate for a period of time, then go out into the world to accomplish the tasks of our lives. When we are upbeat or energized we may even feel like shouting, "ready or not, here I come." Just like hide-and-seek, we will meet with various degrees of success and failure when trying to accomplish our goals. Sometimes we will be lucky or clever enough to look in the right place and meet with success. At other times we will have to look a little longer.

Spiritual practices, of course, have an added dimension to them, something more than just counting and thinking about strategy. Within them, we find God and experience God's grace. This infuses us with a new attitude toward our lives and our desires. When we feel like shouting "ready or not" it will be with other aims in mind. Among them is the desire to bring the results of our reflections and prayers to the world. This may mean to work a little harder on forgiveness, or to be more compassionate toward others. It might just be to remember to take a little bit of the experience of God with us as we go through the day. But just as with hide-and-seek, we will meet with varying degrees of success in these efforts. Living in busy times as we do, our lives have a way of getting away from us. There are a number of distractions, as well as the fact that the world will not always reward even the best of our intentions. Self-centeredness is also a problem.

The interplay between our prayerful moments and the lives we lead in the world is important. It can be both rewarding and frustrating. It is certainly no secret that prayer *is* central to the Christian spiritual life. Jesus often spent time with God in this way. He went up into the mountains to pray after feeding the multitudes (Mark 6:46). He prayed for strength and understanding at the Garden of Gethsemane (Mark 14:35–36). He even prayed when he was on the Cross (Luke 23:34). Saint Paul, too, encouraged prayer, going so far as to advise us to pray continually in 1 Thessalonians 5:17. He also experienced the frustrating aspects of trying to lead a spiritually based life, writing in Romans 7:19 that sometimes he doesn't do the good things he should do but the evil things he *knows* that he should *not* do.

When it comes down to it, there are three main concerns with respect to such practices as prayer and contemplation, including taking the time to do them, determining how to do them, and carrying the results of doing them into the world in a positive way. Making space for time apart with God is more a matter of *discipline* than anything else. An early morning period is a good place to start, which often means getting up a little earlier and spending a few minutes in whatever practice you select. Some difficulties with this are the human tendency to want to sleep as late as possible and the variations in schedule that often take place in our lives. Getting up fifteen minutes earlier is difficult enough, but it is particularly hard after you've had a sleepless night due to worry or because you've been caring for an infant. Add to this the usual changes in routine due to sleeping a little later on the weekends, and you end up with a practice that gets increasingly hard to implement.

There is, of course, little you can do about this other than simply to get up and do your practice. I find that this is similar to exercise. Although the first few minutes may be difficult, it gets easier and more enjoyable once you have started. This makes it easier to do the next day and the day after. The added benefit is that it evens out the variations in your schedule and helps you to deal with the worries and crises that come up in anyone's life.

It is also important to set aside other times during the day for spiritual practice. This helps you to keep from getting carried away by the events of the day. Spending a few minutes later in the morning and in the afternoon in prayer or reading can make a huge difference as far as setting your resolve—and staying reasonably sane!

The next issue has to do with which *method to practice*. There are a multitude of spiritual practices, including centering prayer, meditative scripture reading, and reciting the Lord's Prayer. Each has merit. While I will recommend specific practices later in the book, the bottom line is whether the one you choose allows you better to demonstrate the fruit of the Spirit as found in Galatians 5, that is, love, joy, peace, patience, kindness, generosity, faithfulness, gentleness, and self-control. If after a reasonable period of time you find that you are not growing in any one or more of these areas, then it may be time to move onto something else. I am aware that this goes against the advice some give to stay with a particular method no matter what. Having taken that advice and found more than a few dead ends, I think it best to pursue practices that allow you to keep a spiritual life that includes some variety.

This brings up the final question of carrying over the positive results of your spiritual practice to the rest of the day. I have already mentioned the importance of the fruit of the Spirit in determining whether the spiritual practice you are using is right for you. If you are exhibiting these positive characteristics to a greater degree, then you are succeeding. You would do well to reflect on these once a week to see how you are doing.

Another way of carrying over the results is to erase some of the distinction between private contemplation and public life. Saint Paul said to pray constantly. One way of doing this is to try to recognize and experience the presence of God. Two enormously helpful books in this regard are Brother Lawrence's *Practice of the Presence of God and the Spiritual Maxims* and Jean-Pierre De Caussade's *Sacrament of the Present Moment*. If you haven't read these books, you should! Also read John Ortega's *God Is Closer than You Think* for a contemporary account of such a practice.

In looking at spiritual practices in general, I want to emphasize that they are *not* always going to be easy, and they do *not* guarantee a trouble-free life. One of the great truths, as written by M. Scott Peck in *The Road Less Traveled,* is that life is difficult. Spiritual practices don't make this truth go away. You are going to see tragedies and experience them yourself no matter what. You will face frustration when the best of your advice is ignored by friends and loved ones who subsequently suffer consequences that could have been avoided. You will also have to struggle with your own inclinations and desires, as well as the results of your wrong decisions.

All of this can make you decide to give up and face the world on your own. This can be a conscious decision, but more often than not I think it is an unconscious one. An unfortunate series of events happens, and you end up dealing with life without the benefit of God. You become so stressed that you forget to pray, to read, and to do any of the things that you know have a calming influence upon you and those around you. You forget to experience God's grace.

One way I have learned to look at the world is to see that chaos is an ever-present possibility in life. Unpredictability is at the heart of chaos, so it can strike at any given time and in any given way. There are many possible sources of chaos in our world. You may have to deal with identity theft, with the consequences of a mistake made by one of your family members, or with suddenly finding yourself in a difficult work situation—or out of work altogether! You may have to deal with all of these at once and feel that your world is in complete chaos. These are just a few things that can go wrong.

To confront all of this, it helps to take the time to create space and to fill that space with the love of God. No doubt that space will wax and wane due to circumstances, but it is important to keep creating it. Ready or not, you will have to emerge into the world. Spiritual disciplines, along with finding spiritual people with whom to commune, are enormously important to dealing positively with the unpredictability and chaos that is out there.

This small book on seeking and finding *grace* looks at various ways of experiencing grace and taking the experience, ready or not, into the world. It is a book on Christian spirituality, because it begins and ends with the love of Christ. Certainly some methods and observations are similar to those of other religious traditions. Having experienced the love of Christ firsthand, however, and sought to live within this experience, my bias and understanding begin there. For me, this means five specific things:

1. Accepting Christ's sacrifice for me and his saving grace as a reality in my life.

2. Experiencing the Holy Spirit as I go through the day.

3. Working to extend the kingdom of heaven to others.

4. Loving God and loving others as best as I can.

5. Using the fruit of the Spirit as listed by St. Paul in Galatians 5:22–23 as a means of measuring how I am doing.

This last point is particularly important to me as I go through my life. Manifesting love, joy, peace, patience, kindness, generosity, faithfulness, gentleness, and self-control are the means of seeing how I am doing at any given point of time. It is only through the mystery of God's grace that I am able, in whatever way I can, to give this fruit to a troubled world.

The remaining chapters of this book discuss seven topics with respect to Christian spirituality and how to make this spirituality practical. The subject of the next chapter, *grace*, is important to Christian spirituality because it is how God's love is most experienced. Opening to God's grace is what Christian spirituality is all about. The next chapter looks at *practices* you can put into place to experience God's grace and reflect it to others. *Hope* is the subject of the fourth chapter. Hope is essential in times as trying as ours and in itself is a spiritual practice. It can be hard to be hopeful, particularly when we act as if things should always be perfect and there should never be any natural or unnatural disasters. Hopeful principles help us to stay positive even in trying circumstances.

The subject of the fifth chapter, *self-control*, is a topic that is often overlooked in today's world. As a fruit of the Spirit, it is interesting to see how it plays out in spiritual practice. We will see how it works with respect to work, speech, and interacting with others. Chapter 6 looks at what I call *"mustard-seed thinking."* Jesus tells us that the kingdom of heaven is like a mustard seed that, while small at first, grows enormously (Matt 13:31–32). This chapter discusses how to apply this principle to your life.

Chapter 7 discusses the idea of *community*. Finding a nurturing community can be difficult, particularly for spiritual people who happen to be more introverted than extroverted. Yet it can be done with just a few modifications to your schedule. Since no one can go it entirely alone, it is important to explore ways to enter into the dance of community. The final chapter discusses spiritual transformation through looking at the idea of *holiness*. Holiness might be a lofty goal, but it is one that we can aspire to and draw inspiration from as we grow in the faith.

I end the book with an Annotated Bibliography and an Afterword that introduces it. As you will see at a few places in the book, I believe that reading can be an important part of spiritual development. The Afterword and Annotated Bibliography expand on that belief. I list in the Annotated Bibliography all of the books mentioned in the text that follows, along with several others that in one way or another helped me on my journey. I also include one or two sentences about each book and even list a few Web sites. I hope that these will be a means of helping you to continue down the path toward experiencing a greater sense of God's grace in your daily life.

I want to conclude this introductory chapter with a brief discussion on the differences and similarities between religion and spirituality. This is an important issue with respect to living a grace-filled life in modern times. Some want to lead a spiritual life *outside* of religion. It seems to me that religion is concerned with the practices associated with a particular way of looking at God and God's expectations of us, while spirituality focuses more on the experience of God. Naturally, there is a great deal of overlap here. Attending a church service, for example, is a religious practice as much as it is, or can be, a spiritual one. You can also meditate and pray according to methods specified by a particular religion.

One aspect of spirituality has to do with overcoming perceived shortcomings on the part of organized religion. If you can't seem to find enough of an agreement with any particular religion, or feel that all religions are seriously flawed in some way, but still claim an experience with God, then you might say that you are a spiritual person but not a religious one. It would be hard to say, however, that someone could be religious and *not* spiritual, since religion itself involves claims about God and our ability to understand and experience God.

Of course, all earthly institutions have flaws and can be condemned by others for one reason or another. On the other hand, humans, being social creatures, tend to congregate together and search for others with similar attitudes and beliefs. My own bias is to practice spirituality within the Christian religion and, further than that, within a church setting. I find that expressing and working through differences of viewpoint only help to deepen my faith and my spiritual experience. And, seeing everyone as human and, therefore, flawed in some way, I don't expect to find anyone in church who isn't struggling with something. My spiritual practice would be impoverished if I only worshiped with people who thought and acted exactly as I do, or wish I did.

As you read this book, I encourage you to search your heart and mind for ways that you can use these words to deepen your knowledge of God both in a religious *and* a spiritual way. Consider ways that you can experience God's grace through such practices as prayer and contemplation. Consider, too, how you can take the results of such practices, ready or not, into the world.

CHAPTER TWO
Grace

Recently I was in Boston attending a conference. During one of the breaks, I walked to a nearby bookstore and purchased a small notebook so I could jot down a few personal thoughts. Afterward, I went over to a park and sat down on a bench beneath a shade tree. While there, I experienced a wonderful sense of peace. It was as if everything in the world had slowed down. I felt a deep sense of kinship to those walking by me. It was a connection to others that I must admit I don't often feel.

I experienced grace in a different setting shortly thereafter. When I returned from Boston I argued with one of my children over something that had happened while I was away. Although I am usually agitated in such circumstances, I recognized a sense of peace here as well. This kept the argument from escalating and allowed us to reach a good understanding. The feeling of "grace under pressure" kept me from overreacting.

Grace is a word that is hard to pin down. In the two instances above, it involved a sense of peace and well-being. It may be experienced during times of solitude, ordinary activity, or conflict. A feeling of connectedness may also be present—a connectedness to God and to others.

For Christians, grace is part of our relationship with God. I believe that it is extended to us to help us overcome a sense of separateness from God and from one another. When we follow our tendencies toward self-centeredness we manifest unfortunate symptoms of this separateness. We become overly concerned with ourselves and with our reputations. Anger, fear, greed, and pride are just some of the attributes that go along with an ungraceful existence.

Of course, grace is a fundamental part of our forgiveness. When I was younger, I used to wonder about this process. Had I really done anything so bad that it warranted forgiveness? Doesn't this embody an overly negative view of human nature? Now that I am older I see the many ways in which my own self-centeredness gets in the way. I can't even go to the store for someone without picking something out for myself as well. Not to do so would be a waste of my time.

The phrase "in spite of" typifies the standard view of grace. *God loves us in spite of the fact that we only think of ourselves.* We are loved in spite of the fact that we often don't want to help others and could never do enough to warrant what God has bestowed upon us. Grace is more than this, however. It is not only the process of forgiveness; it is the *feeling* of forgiveness as well. It involves the knowledge that we are favored in God's eyes. It is also the experience of God's love even in the most mundane experiences of everyday life.

Christian spirituality breathes in the air of God's grace. Spirituality is the way in which we experience the love of God and reflect that love to others. Grace is extended to us so that we may experience this love. It is around us in the good times as well as in the bad. It is an ever-present reality possible for us to know.

Getting at the experience of this grace is a highly individualized process. People are very different and have different struggles, weaknesses, and strengths. Some people seem to reflect God's grace easily and don't need to work hard at it. Others have a more difficult time experiencing it and have to work at it.

One way of determining what you need to do to experience more of God's grace and to grow spiritually is simply to look at the people around you. Who are the people that have a deep spiritual presence about them? Are there activities that they do that you can also put into practice? Another possibility is to notice people who are similar to you in temperament. If you were to counsel them on how to grow spiritually, what would you advise?

Another suggestion is to seek out people who may be able to offer you spiritual guidance. The path of spiritual guidance is, of course, tricky and can be filled with promises and pitfalls. You don't want to rely totally on any one person to be the ultimate example of spiritual living for you. Christ alone has that quality. Still, spiritual guidance can be an excellent means of getting to grace.

One aspect of experiencing grace has to do with getting beyond the difficult times that all of us will inevitably face. During such periods, it is easy to wallow in pity and self-blame. Moreover, people in your environment are more than willing to allow you to engage in the self-blame game. They'll tell you that you should have acted a certain way. Had you done that, things would have turned out differently. I've caught myself doing this with my own children. You may also suffer from the irrational feeling that you are the only one that has ever faced a particular problem. Your self-recrimination prevents you from seeing that whatever problem you are facing has been faced by others as well. But remember: *You are not alone.*

A good analogy for dealing with this particular type of situation comes from the computer world. I have spent hours trying to fix something related to my computer, unconsciously thinking that I am the only person who has had this problem. Surely it has to do with some mistake I made in loading new software or running a program. The Internet and the magic of search engines taught me how irrational such a belief is. I can simply go to one of the search engines and enter in some words that explain whatever computer problem I am having. The result is usually a number of "hits" on technology forums and other places that indicate how common the problem is. Many also offer solutions. This approach saves me hours of work. It teaches me something far more valuable as well: Other people have faced whatever problem I am having, whether it is financial, personal, or emotional. Searching the problem on the Internet helps me to see this and also helps me to see possible solutions.

How does this apply to grace? The blame-game makes me feel unworthy in many respects. Seeing that others have faced a similar problem eases the burden somewhat. It creates a crack where the light of grace can shine through. It teaches me the humility necessary to understanding that I am *not* perfect, that I make mistakes, and that these mistakes can either have solutions or can be dealt with in some form or fashion. Once I get beyond that, I can experience the love of God in my daily life. *That* is grace.

One other aspect of grace has to do with the fact that sometimes you feel more of it than at other times. There seems to be an ebb and flow of grace. The periods of high and low grace can be quite lengthy. I find that periods of low grace can be eased by a change in spiritual practice or attitude. A friend of mine named Brian, for example, was in a situation where he had to take care of his aging parents one day a week. He resented this time, and his resentment spilled over into other areas of life. Grace was not a feeling he experienced. In looking at the situation, he discovered that his parents simply lived in a world that was slower than his. He was usually racing around at a hundred miles an hour while his parents were moving at fifteen!

He handled this situation by making a conscious effort to slow down when he was around them. He took a few minutes to prepare himself mentally before entering their world. He even took this on as a spiritual practice. Once he did so, he found that he was able to enjoy his time with his parents much more easily. He began to cherish the time he spent with them, moving at a slower pace and taking the time to see things that he ordinarily would not notice. This is not to say that his time with them always goes smoothly. There are still occasions when he gets a little frustrated with the way they see the world. Still, he has a much better time of it now that he has learned to move according to their clock.

Brian transferred this slowness to his regular world as well. He took a Christian-influenced exercise class that involved slow-stretching exercises. It seems that grace is often found by moving a little more slowly, and Brian began to find more grace-filled moments. This was all from the result of what he once recognized as an irritant in his life.

It's hard to say whether the ebb and flow of grace comes from God or whether it is a result of something else. It is possible to change your behavior and attitude in order to find a closer relationship with God and God's grace. When I have done this, more often than not, it *has* worked.

Why doesn't God grant us the feeling of grace all of the time? The short answer is that grace is largely experienced through faith. If we experienced grace all of the time, there would be no need for faith. We would all be believers. *Faith* is required of most of us *before* the experience of grace comes along. One reason behind this is that God made us to be creatures with free will. The British philosopher and theologian Richard Swinburne explores the logic behind this in his work. His books, *The Existence of God* and *The Resurrection of God Incarnate*, are examples of his highly reasoned approach. His writing style is very sophisticated, and his arguments would be impossible for me to reproduce here in any level of detail. Suffice it to say that according to Swinburne there is no *deductive* proof for the existence of God. In other words, there is not an irrefutable argument for God's existence. Reasonable and intelligent people can believe that there is no God and still be counted as reasonable and intelligent. There is, however, a strong *inductive* argument for God's existence. Unlike deductive logic, which deals in certainties, inductive logic deals in probabilities and percentages.

Weather prediction is perhaps the most easily understood analogy here. A meteorologist might say that, given current conditions, there is an 80 percent chance of rain tomorrow. This is not to say that it will definitely rain. Instead, based upon a number of factors, it is more likely to rain tomorrow than it is likely not to rain. Swinburne argues that such factors as the predictability of the universe and the moral sensibilities of people point to the possibility of the existence of God. Moreover, it is probable that the type of God that exists would create people with the ability to choose their beliefs. They can either decide to put faith in God and experience grace or reject the existence of God. This is the "logic of grace," if you will.

There is one other aspect of spirituality and grace that I would like to touch on before we go to the next topic. This has to do with the misconception that spirituality necessarily leads one *away* from social action. Several factors may lead to this conclusion. Meditation, centering prayer, and other such practices that people use to experience grace do take time away from otherwise acting in the world. Moreover, the people who are attracted to such practices are likely to be more introverted than extroverted.

While it is true that a person can spend an excessive amount of time gazing at his or her navel and not doing anything for other people, there is an important sense in which spiritual practices are necessary to good social action. It takes a fairly refined understanding of God and the world to act positively within it. We would not accuse Gandhi of excessive meditation, although he was a spiritual man who engaged in spiritual practices. Nor would we accuse Martin Luther King, Jr. of being removed from the world, although he was a man of prayer. Jesus himself is a good model here, for he both practiced prayer and acted in the world. He healed the sick (Matt 4:23), fed the hungry (Mark 8:1–9), and advised his disciples to give to the poor (Luke 12:33), just as he spent time in prayer (Mark 1:35).

Grace in this context provides us with the insight to act in the world in positive ways. The spiritual practices through which grace is experienced also provide us with enough detachment to keep our energy levels high and our minds clear. Becoming too caught up in a situation can wreak havoc on a person's sense of balance. Dealing with an addict, for example, requires a large sense of perspective and calm. Having dealt with a number of people who suffer from a variety of addictions, I know that it is important to maintain a sense of detachment. Without this you are likely to be on an emotional roller coaster. This is one reason why spirituality is such a huge part of successful twelve-step programs for addicts, as well as for those who must work with addicts. Understanding that there are things that we can't control and giving things over to a "higher power" is as important for the addict as it is for those that love and care for the addict. Such understanding springs from a spiritual and grace-filled understanding of God.

Grace is a good place to start any discussion of Christian spirituality. In many respects, it is what makes our faith unique. Grace itself is a multifaceted word with subtleties of meaning. It is something more easily experienced than explained. It is fundamental to our experience of God, for through it we realize that *God forgives us no matter who we are or what we have done.* This sense of forgiveness brings along with it a powerful sense of the love of God. This is a love that can be experienced in both the quiet and active moments of the day. Rather than encouraging a reserved approach to the world, grace can and should inform action that works to help others. This is our way of extending the kingdom of heaven to others. It can also help us to see where injustices have occurred, either individually or socially, and take action to correct them. Finally, grace helps us to deal with the good times and people in our lives, as well as with the more difficult times and people. Grace, along with consistent spiritual practice, opens the door for us to do what we must do in order to be God's servants here on earth.

CHAPTER THREE
Practicing Spirituality

*T*he other night I had the opportunity to watch the movie Radio, once again. Released in 2003, it tells the true story of a mentally handicapped African American man in a small town in South Carolina. The local high school football coach takes the young man under his wing and involves him in the school's activities. Not knowing the man's name at first, the coach dubs him "Radio" due to his love of transistor radios.

The coach is criticized by one of the more influential football booster club members for allowing Radio on the sidelines during the games, and is questioned by school administrators for encouraging his attendance in school. The coach persists, and he and Radio ultimately succeed in winning everyone over to seeing the good of allowing him to be a part of the school.

I summarize the movie not because I feel that it was the best movie ever made (far from it). The plot has flaws and the actual events of the story have been altered somewhat to fit Hollywood formulas. The story is remarkable, however, in at least one respect. It is a staggering account of how to do good in the face of opposition. Needless to say, we don't get many such depictions in today's movies. I had a humbling realization as the movie unfolded: We should all be like the coach.

What does this have to do with practicing spirituality? The point is that one of the primary measures of our lives as Christians is the way that we act. It isn't how much time we spend meditating or reading the Bible, or whether such activities lower blood pressure or prolong life. We need to be good people and to love one another. The love of others should be our primary concern. All of our talents, abilities, and attributes are worthless without love.

It is essential that a book on spirituality and grace mentions practices that help to lead a grace-filled life. Below is a rather simple method that I have developed. It is not comprehensive in scope, and there are certainly other practices you could use that would have equal results. The bottom line with respect to the movie is that if you can lead a good life without a set spiritual practice that you follow every day, then that's fine. If you think that a spiritual method such as the one below might help, then please consider using it.

I have already mentioned that St. Paul in Thessalonians encourages us to pray without ceasing (1 Thess 5:17). As I was putting this method together and trying to think of an acronym that would be memorable, the word *PRAYER* came to mind. Each of the letters corresponds to a word that is important to the spiritual life and can be put into practice on a daily basis. The first letter (P) actually stands for *Prayer*. The second letter (R) stands for *Reading*. Reading the Bible and other spiritually based texts can have an enormous influence on your life. *Action* (A) is close to the center of the word and is, of course, where the fruit of the Spirit is most displayed. *Yielding* (Y) is something that we should all do throughout the day, and is also a part of acting. *Exercise* (E) is perhaps the most unusual and more modern of the ideas I include in this acronym, so I will need to spend a little time explaining that. Finally, *Relaxation* (R) covers the ideas of spending time both in meditation or communion with God, as well as reflecting upon where you are in your spiritual life.

Prayer is probably the best known and most practiced of the Christian spiritual disciplines. It is easy to do and can be done in all manner of ways. There are so many good books on prayer that I won't even bother recommending one here, but be certain to see my Annotated Bibliography at the end of this book.

Three types of prayer that I want to mention are (1) communion prayers, (2) traditional prayers, and (3) prayers of supplication.

Prayers of communion are those where the person praying desires to be closer to God. *Centering prayer* is an example. This is where the person praying selects a meaningful word and meditates upon it for twenty minutes once or twice a day. The word *Abba*, meaning *father*, is one that I have used for this purpose. Other types of communion prayers involve simply thinking about the image of God for a period of time or contemplating God's love. The point of all of these is to be close to God and to feel God's love.

A second type of prayer is *traditional prayer*. The Lord's Prayer (the Our Father) is the most widely known and practiced. The Prayer of St. Francis, another such prayer; begins, "Lord, make me an instrument of Thy peace," and can be found at the end of this book. These prayers have been around for centuries and are good at helping you to find your center during good and bad times. They may also be used for communion purposes through reflecting on the words. Great insights can result from simply praying the Lord's Prayer, for example.

The third type of prayer is that of *supplication*. This is when we are asking God to provide aid in a particular situation, such as a healing. It is very natural for us to turn to God in the face of illness or tragedy. Difficulties may arise when the tragedy is *not* abated and the illness is *not* healed. Nevertheless, the Bible says that we can and should turn to God during such instances (Jas 5:13–18). In the end, what we must do is to give the situation over to God. A good method for praying for healing is inspired by one I found in the writings of Agnes Sanford, who wrote such classics on healing and prayer as *The Healing Light*. In this method, you find a quiet place and wait a moment to experience God's presence. Then ask for God's help and picture in your mind God's actually bringing about the result you desire. See the person being healed. Thank God for the healing, and then acknowledge that God's will be done and end the prayer. This method may also be used for dealing with difficult situations.

As far as time of day is concerned, it is important to begin and end each day with prayer. This is true no matter what method of prayer you choose. Set aside a few minutes in the early morning to be with God, and end your day thanking God for God's blessings.

Reading the scriptures is as important as prayer is in the life of a Christian, and represents the second aspect of the spiritual life. Reflective reading is where we can discover God's will for us. The amazing thing about the Bible is that it actually speaks to us through slow reading and reflection. We learn from the various situations people of the Bible faced, as well as from the inspiration and advice God's writers have given to others. Read the Bible as if it were written just for you because, in point of fact, it was! Try not to let a day go by without turning to the Bible, even if it is just to read a verse or two. Turn the verses over in your mind a couple of times as you go through your day.

It is also good to read other spiritually based words of wisdom, advice, inspiration, or elucidation. If you like to read, as I do, then this is fairly easy to do. There are also a large number of good books from which to choose (see the Annotated Bibliography). I recently discovered John Ortega's books, for example, and have profited enormously from them. Such authors help you to consider new ways of encountering God. Granted, some people don't like to read and will have some difficulty with this. Being a voracious reader is not a necessary requirement of the spiritual life, however. If reading a few lines of scripture is all you have the time or desire to do, then don't feel badly about it. Read your scripture and move on. You might try a spiritual book occasionally just to add some variety to your reading.

I already mentioned the importance of *Acting* to spiritual practice when I talked about the movie *Radio*. Acting in the world is where you see the fruits of your practice. From a spiritual perspective, the best thing that you can do is to remember to keep God with you throughout your day. This, of course, is easier said than done. It is easy to get caught up in the circumstances of life.

Helpful at the beginning of your day is to ask God to be with you throughout it. Make it a habit to check in with God periodically so that you feel God's presence. Another method is simply to be attuned to your breathing. You will notice that when you are stressed your breathing becomes shallow. When you experience this, pause and take some deep breaths and remind yourself that God is there with you. Another approach is simply to slow down in whatever activity you are doing and give your full attention to it in a God-centered way. Too often we are doing one thing while also thinking about what we will do next. Slowing down and focusing on whatever you are doing make it easier to include God in the activity. Whether I am writing or working in the yard, I find that it helps to share the activity with God. This makes an enormous difference.

Most importantly, look for ways that you can *help others throughout the day*. Sometimes these moments come unexpectedly, but often you will have to plan them. Think of an individual or a group of people you can help, and then do it. This can be as easy as calling someone that you know is having difficulty, or taking the time to talk to your son or daughter. Bear in mind that your good action doesn't always have to be toward someone outside of your family or your immediate environment. But when it does come to moving beyond your circle of friends and family, look for God's will for you. For example, I seem to have a special love for young people, and know that at some point I will need to do something in that area to honor God's will for me. Look for similar messages in your own life.

Yielding is another one of those central activities that is related to acting with God's presence. It involves planned moments when you give yourself over to God. It need only take a minute or two and can be done in between activities and appointments. All you have to do is to take a minute or two at a few points during the day and offer yourself and your activities to God.

While I am on the subject of yielding, I'd like to provide you with an insight that was given to me by a friend many years ago. I was in my early thirties and still trying to find what I could do for God. I was looking for something big, such as dedicating myself to end world hunger, while at the same time knowing that I had to provide for my own young family. I was very frustrated and mentioned this to a friend.

"Are you yielding in small things?" he asked. "If you are not yielding in small things, then you can't expect God to give you big things to work on."

His statement took me by surprise. I reflected on my life and realized that I wasn't yielding in small things. In fact, most of my day was spent thinking about myself and ignoring God and others entirely. I hardly took the time to think about God, except when I was expressing frustration over not knowing exactly what I was supposed to do with my life. I realized at that point that if I was going to do God's work, I needed to train myself to yield in ways both large and small.

The next method, *Exercise*, is one that may take you by surprise. Exercise is hardly mentioned in the Bible, and is not something people tend to associate with loving God. At the same time, I think it is important to leading a balanced life. Study after study shows the benefits of exercise in terms of improving health and enhancing mental abilities. As a country, the United States has become too sedentary, as is evidenced by our growing waistlines. People who exercise tend to feel and think better. Clear thinking is helpful in dealing with stress, as well as in improving your relationship with God.

Exercise can become explicitly God-relational by your including God in whatever activity you undertake. You can walk or run, for example, and think about God while doing so. Of course, you also need to focus on your environment for safety purposes. Regardless of whatever activity you undertake, do it for the sake of keeping your stress under control so that you can better serve God.

Relaxation is the last of our recommendations. This involves simply being with God in a relaxed state. Spend some time opening yourself to God and enjoying God's wonder. I find that this is especially helpful in the early evening as well as upon going to bed. Similar to exercise, it is essential to freeing yourself from stress. You can also spend some time reflecting upon your day and thinking about how you can better serve God tomorrow.

I tend to follow the activities of PRAYER sequentially. I spend time in the morning in prayer and reading, include God in my actions throughout the day, take particular times to yield to God, exercise either in the afternoon or early evening, and relax and reflect upon God at the end of the day. This is not necessarily the sequence that *you* have to follow, and I change it myself from time to time to fit my schedule. The point is that you can take each of these six elements and fit them to your own schedule and temperament. There is also endless variation within each of the recommendations. There are a number of ways to pray, a number of inspirational books to read, different ways you can include God in your activities, and so forth. This method can be a quick "report card" of sorts to see how you are doing. I write PRAYER on a card that I keep in my wallet and pull it out occasionally to ask myself how I am doing with respect to each of the activities.

As with anything, it is important not to let the activities above, either separately or collectively, become the sole focus of your existence. Most importantly, we are called to love God and others. Don't allow *any* method to get in the way of that.

The story of *Radio* is an example of how one man came to practice love. It is an example of how at times we need to go against convention and the opinions of others in order to do the right thing. It helps to see such examples so that we can think about how we can reflect the love of God to others. Following such examples, and practicing spiritual disciplines, is a way of increasing God's presence in our lives. This is as much a joy as it is a challenge.

CHAPTER FOUR
Being Hopeful

*T*here was a time when I dreaded going to the mailbox. I was handling some significant issues for various members of my family. Some were legal, some financial, and some medical. Many involved correspondence of one sort or another. My daily trip to check the mail was filled with trepidation. Since the problems involved others and not me, I felt powerless and more than a little resentful. Dealing with my own problems was hard enough. Dealing with the problems of others contained added dimensions of difficulty.

The situation eased a bit as time progressed. Some of the problems went away, while others became more manageable. I found that effectively handling the problems meant that I needed to change in important ways. For example, I needed to think about my relationships with others. When my wife and I had children I promised myself that I would never be one of those parents who constantly complain about them. Yet I had become just that! I also had to look at the way I felt about handling the affairs of others. I needed to gain confidence in my decision-making and learn to give to God what I cannot control. In all this, I also needed to find hope.

Hope is an important part of spirituality. It's hard to be spiritual if you don't have hope. It's also difficult to practice loving God and loving others if you are depressed or lack a positive view of the future. Of course, without hope it's hard to practice much of anything.

There is a deep sense in which hope is part of Christian spirituality. We have hope in the future and in the life that is to come. Hope is part of the view that no matter what happens here, we can put our hope in Christ that things will work out, if not in this world, then in the next. Ultimately, hope is part of our belief in the mission of Christ to love, forgive, and redeem us.

This view of hope is well-documented in the Bible. We are told to put our hope in God and that hope in Christ will help us to endure. There are some instances in the New Testament where faith, hope, and love are mentioned together. Although St. Paul tells us in 1 Corinthians 13:13 that love is the better of the three "theological virtues," hope is important. These three virtues are inextricably linked in that faith creates hope in the present and the future. Faith and hope help us to practice the love of God and of others, which is the most important of the spiritual gifts.

What can we say about such hope in the face of the inevitable difficulties of life? There are certainly times when all of us feel far from hopeful. Some particularly troubling event comes along that captures all of our attention and makes us see everything in a dim light. We question our decisions and wonder if there will ever be a time when things are OK.

Battling such hopelessness is by no means an easy task. I don't think it helps simply to say that Christians should never feel such things. We are, after all, human and subject to human frailties, including tendencies toward hopelessness and depression when things aren't going our way. I believe that it helps to see such instances as traumas from which you will heal. Allow yourself time to experience the anger or sadness you may feel. But while you are doing so, start to pray about it, learning to give the situation to God. Be sure to seek out others who can help you, whether they are friends or trained professionals. After some time has passed, find your way to hope again, remembering that whatever problem you are facing is limited by space and time while God's love is unlimited. You can find hope through leaning on Jesus and the Holy Spirit in even the most difficult situations.

There is one view of hope and belief that I want to comment on even though I haven't totally worked out my own opinion of it yet. This is the view of Wayne Dyer and others that if you believe in the abundance of God and the world, then good things are bound to happen to you. Florence Shinn is a Christian writer of the last century with a similar viewpoint. The idea is that if you need something and totally trust in God, then God will provide what you need and will respond to your wishes. If you have just lost your job and need $500 to pay the rent, for example, you can put your hope, faith, and trust in God and God's abundance and the money will come to you.

This is a difficult topic for me because part of me wants to believe it, while another part has a hard time accepting it as true. Certainly there are scriptural references that indicate that whatever we ask for God will provide. Jesus says that, "whatever you ask for in prayer, believe that you have received it, and it will be yours" (Mark 11:24). The numerous healings that Jesus did during his ministry also attest to the power of faith and prayer. On the other hand, we know that St. Paul had an affliction, a "thorn," which he prayed about and which was *not* taken away (2 Cor 12:7–9). Jesus himself prayed for the cup to pass by him in the Garden of Gethsemane, and *that* was not granted (Matt 26:39). I am also sure that many of Jesus' disciples as well as Christian martyrs over the centuries, all obviously people of great faith, prayed for God's deliverance from persecution but were not spared.

What we are talking about here is hope that a particular thing will take place. This may be hope for money to cover an expense, for the healing of a loved one, or for something either to come into or leave your life. I believe that writers like Wayne Dyer and Florence Shinn are onto something when they say that believing something will happen increases the probability that it will take place. If anything, deep belief will cause you to act in such a way as to better attract whatever it is you want into your life. As with anything, you can go too far with this. If you want to learn Spanish, for example, or earn a medical degree, prayer alone won't bring these about. There has to be some effort involved. Prayer also won't change what ultimately proves to be God's will. Still, a positive attitude, *an attitude of belief,* will certainly contribute to whatever you want to accomplish and may even help attract something you desire into your life.

One response to this could be that all things work to the good for those who love God. This is also a way of interpreting "thy will be done" in the Lord's Prayer. In other words, learn to see whatever happens in life as ultimately God's will, which we don't fully understand. For example, the sickness a child has, may be bad in the short term, but (provided the child recovers) may help that child to build immunities against future illnesses that may be even worse. To take another example, a legal charge against someone who has a behavioral issue may bring significant short-term problems, but may be just the thing needed for that individual to decide to change. This view helps to some extent, although we know that sometimes children die as a result of illness and sometimes people fail to change even after bad things happen to them.

I guess I am somewhere in the middle when it comes to the power of faith and hope. I would like to be able to say that if you simply believe long and hard enough, then things will always work out in your favor. That is certainly a popular message and one that is easy to convey. I have no doubt that if you put your love and faith in God that great things will happen. Some of them will be things that you really want to happen. I also believe that if you see in your mind what you want to accomplish and include God in the image, then you will immeasurably increase the probability that you will get it. There is something to this faith business. Just don't expect life always to work out for you in the way that you would like—bad things happen. Even Wayne Dyer has had to go through the pain of divorce. Although he seems to have handled such losses well, they no doubt presented difficulties.

Being hopeful about the daily affairs of life ultimately means hoping for the best, acting on the belief that the best will happen, and trusting the rest to God. There are some ways of being hopeful that are particularly helpful. The first is to be positive and hopeful even if you don't want to. Defy your doubts that life can be better. When you hear about someone taking on a positive frame of mind, and then something positive happening as a result, you may be inclined to think that it might work for someone *else* but not for *you*. Or, you may feel that someone has mistakenly taken a single instance of something good happening and turned it into a universal law.

I encourage you to suspend such thinking for a time. After all, if you get up in the morning expecting good things to happen and they don't, what real harm has been done? Life consists of both the actual events that take place and our reactions to them. Looking for the good even in "negative" situations can actually lead to good things taking place. Try it and find out.

Another approach is to have quick reminders to help you refocus. Try carrying something around that helps to remind you of God's love. Write down a piece of scripture that is meaningful to you and read it on occasion. Remember, too, that some of your "natural" tendencies during difficult times may not be particularly effective. Excessive worry, for example, often does more harm than good. Read Jesus' Sermon on the Mount in Matthew (5—7) and pay close attention to what he says about the futility of worry. Write some of these verses down and use them to help you stay focused in the present.

A third approach is simply to practice ways of staying connected to God. Suspend your worry during difficult times, and don't let negative thinking keep you from prayer. Avoid too much self-blame for the mistakes of your past. Try to find practical advice that helps you to do this. One statement I agree with in Mitch Albom's *The Five People You Meet in Heaven* is that *all* parents damage their children in some way. That statement helps me to overcome the feeling that I should have been a perfect parent. There is nothing wrong with trying to be the best parent you can be, but realize that *no one* is perfect. Your imperfections are going to have consequences, especially in family situations. My tendency to be overprotective and worry, for example, created a bit of a rebellious streak in my children, or so they tell me. It would have been far better if I had managed to combine the right amount of parental concern with the right amount of freedom, but that was beyond my abilities. For me, staying connected to God means not being overcome with guilt for my perceived failures. It also means praying for hope in good and bad situations, and looking for God's guidance and wisdom throughout.

Hope is one of the distinguishing characteristics of the Christian spiritual life. We have hope as the result of the power of the Holy Spirit and through our knowledge of Jesus' life and ministry. Being hopeful is hard in the face of the tragedies and difficulties of everyday life. In such situations Jesus asks us to take the larger perspective. We are to see that God is bigger than the problems that confront us. This is almost impossible to do in a society such as ours that rejects pain and acts as if nothing bad should ever happen. Often people feel that the government should step in and erase whatever mishap may have occurred. Certainly there are some obligations that a democratic government has, but ensuring that nothing bad ever happens to anyone isn't one of those obligations. Nothing on earth can prevent bad things from happening to good people—or to *any* type of person for that matter. What we *can* do during difficult times is rely on our faith that *this* is not all that there is.

Being hopeful is hard, but it is also powerful. When I was researching and writing a book on prayer and healing, I was impressed by the many stories I heard about the effectiveness of prayer. I continued to hear such stories even after the book was published. I came away from this experience convinced about the power of prayer. Just asking a few questions to a group of people usually unlocks truly miraculous experiences. Sometimes we focus too much on instances when something such as prayer doesn't work. Yet changing your perspective can yield truly amazing results. When you look for examples of miracles, you will begin to see them everywhere.

"Changing perspective" is where I would like to end this discussion. We have a measure of freedom with respect to how we view the world. Interestingly, the world often conforms to how we view it. If we anticipate that things will go wrong, then we'll take notice when they do. If something good happens, we will see it as an exception. Yet we can turn things around and see just the opposite happening. We can take on an attitude where we see the good things that happen as the norm and the bad as the exception. Taking such an attitude, which I see as the essence of hope, has many benefits. You can even take this attitude further. Research on "luck," as recounted in such books as Richard Wiseman's *The Luck Factor*, indicates that people who see themselves as lucky have an unusual talent. They are able to take negative experiences and find the good in them. A minor car accident, for example, becomes a chance to meet someone who will bring a new perspective or a new opportunity.

Being hopeful is perhaps one of the most difficult spiritual practices that one can undertake in a world such as ours. It can be fostered through prayer, reading, and attention to your attitude. It doesn't help to be *mindlessly* hopeful, because that simply isn't realistic and is often irritating to others. A quiet, constant hopefulness can, however, make a difference in your life and in that of those around you. Hope creates the endurance and positive attitude needed to be a positive influence in the world. The New Testament writers knew this, and we can know this as well. The world needs people who are capable of being hopeful and who are able to use that hope for the benefit of others.

CHAPTER FIVE
Self-Control

Jim had developed the habit of having a few drinks at the end of each week. Since he never got quite drunk, he saw this as a fairly harmless way of releasing stress at the end of the day on Friday. This really wasn't a problem until his son, Justin, reached adolescence. As he moved into his teen years, Justin became something of a difficult child who was as headstrong as he was vocal. Jim was able to deal with Justin effectively when he was stone cold sober. The effects of a few drinks, however, took away his coolness and made Jim as emotional as Justin was argumentative. Friday nights became stressful as Jim lost his temper at Justin's sarcastic *comments and demands. Jim's wife, Kathy, was barely able to keep the peace between them.*

It didn't take Jim long to see that alcohol was not something he should be bringing into a difficult situation. Dealing with Justin required a great deal of coolheadedness, and even a small amount of liquor took that away. What was lacking on the part of both Jim and Justin was *self-control*. Although Jim couldn't force his son to exhibit self-control, he could do something about his own lack of it by simply not drinking. He had to exercise self-control by not consuming alcohol so that he could also control himself with Justin.

Self-control is a virtue that is difficult to sustain in our society. Everywhere we look there are examples of self-indulgence. Alcoholism and drug abuse rates are high, as are divorce rates. Premarital and extramarital sex are the norm, and television programs and movies now have plots and scenes that would have been unthinkable years ago. The irony is that people such as Madonna, who made their fortunes pushing the envelope as far as perceptions of public decency are concerned, now carefully monitor what their own children watch on television!

In short, self-control is not a popular concept. Yet it is a Christian one. Self-control is a fruit of the Spirit as listed by St. Paul in Galatians (5:22–23). In writing about spirituality, it is tempting to focus on the other fruit. Who *doesn't* want to think about such things as love, joy, and peace? These are ideas that are pleasant to think about. Self-control is another matter. It can quickly become an uncomfortable topic. Self-control, however, is needed if we are to grow spiritually and to interact with others in a grace-filled way.

To understand self-control, it helps to compare it with the works of the flesh, which St. Paul lists immediately before the fruit of the Spirit (Gal 5:19–21). These are "fornication, impurity, licentiousness, idolatry, sorcery, enmities, strife, jealousy, anger, quarrels, dissensions, factions, envy, drunkenness, carousing, and things like these." Notice how each, to one degree or another, involves *the lack of self-control*. Doing simply what may feel good at the moment results in all manner of depraved and impure activities.

How does self-control work as a fruit of the Spirit? A simple answer would be that following Christ results in a person being able to have total control over such desires. It doesn't appear to be a quick process for most of us though. One doesn't become a Christian and have all immoral desires completely erased. There seems to be more of a growing process involved. All of us are likely to be fortunate enough to know people who are particularly good, virtuous, or whatever other adjective you would use to describe them. You wouldn't dream of seeing such people drunk or engaging in sexual licentiousness. They don't tell off-color jokes or indulge in "adult entertainment." These people would typically be described as *mature* in their faith. They are individuals who have been Christians for some time and who have experienced a growth process. They may have struggled with something in the past, but were able to overcome it as their faith deepened.

We can grow spiritually as a result of watching such people and learning from them. It is also important to remember the metaphor of spirituality as a fruit. Apples don't come out of a tree complete. They grow from buds and age until they are ripened. The same is true of those traits associated with spirituality.

To understand self-control further, it helps to look at biblical examples. The Old Testament contains many stories showing the difficulties caused by a lack of control as well as the good fortune created by self-control. Sodom and Gomorrah were destroyed by God as a result of a lack of self-control on the part of the people who lived there (Gen 13:13; 19:24). King David received great blessings when following God's laws (2 Sam 7:8–17), but experienced tragedy when he went against them (2 Sam 12:9–15). The same is true of other Old Testament figures.

The New Testament also provides positive and negative examples of self-control. Jesus confronts the lack of control in others when he overturns the tables of the money changers in the temple (Mark 11:15) and when he speaks to the woman at the well (John 4:7–30). St. Paul's letters contain diatribes against the lack of control in some of the churches and cities he visited (1 Cor 5:1–2; Eph 5:3–18). On the positive side, Jesus' period in the desert shows his ability to stay in control in spite of enormous temptation (Matt 4:1–11). Similarly, he was able to do God's will during the extreme conditions of the passion (Matt 27:1–54). The disciples also showed self-control and courage in their activities following Jesus' death and resurrection (Acts 5:27–42). It is not implausible to attribute the difference in the nature of the disciples after Jesus' resurrection and ascension into heaven to the work of the Holy Spirit. The last days of Jesus found the disciples scattered with one of the more prominent among them, St. Peter, denying that he even knew Jesus (Matt 26:69–75). The period after Jesus' resurrection has the disciples and St. Paul undertaking acts of courage and sacrifice in the face of danger, acts requiring enormous self-control.

As Christians, it may be helpful to see the Old Testament as providing the basis for understanding the expectations and benefits of self-control and doing God's will, and the New Testament as creating a Christian understanding of self-control as part of the works of the Holy Spirit. This is, of course, a gross oversimplification, but it does capture something of the spirit of the two sections of the Bible. The biblical examples don't provide us everything we need to know with respect to self-control. We face somewhat different temptations in modern times, and have more scientifically based views of human nature. We have to look outside of the Bible for specific advice on how to deal with gambling addictions, for example, or to find proven ways of dealing with substance abuse.

Even with that, it is often the case that effective responses to the lack of self-control have spiritual components to them. Turning to God can help even purely scientific or medical processes. We all know that twelve-step programs rely in large degree upon an understanding that there is a higher being.

I will not address further the issue of what to do about serious problems with self-control, such as drug and other addictions. I lack the qualifications to discuss such issues, and there is already a wealth of information available. Anne M. Fletcher's *Sober for Good*, for example, contains information gleaned from problem drinkers who have quit, as well as overviews of various approaches to dealing with alcoholism. Instead, I will discuss self-control issues faced by individuals not so deeply afflicted.

To begin with, it helps to see where, as a Christian, you are likely to have self-control already working in your life. Many Christians are not at all tempted by pornography and find it generally abhorrent. Others can easily resist drugs and alcohol even though they may have enjoyed the short-term feeling associated with them in the past. They have a quiet strength that enables them to resist such substances. Lacking such desire can and should be recognized, with gratefulness, as instances of self-control.

Once you recognize such instances and express gratefulness for them, you can then take a look at the gaps in your life. Where would you like to exhibit greater self-control in your life? Most of us are acutely aware of these gaps or areas of concern. We tend to feel a sense of guilt after succumbing to a desire in one of these areas. Perhaps you lack self-control when it comes to your eating habits, for example, and feel badly when you have eaten too much. Or maybe you like to engage in gossip about people and feel guilty after doing so.

Recognition that you have a problem is, of course, the first step in overcoming it. Once you realize that there is an area where you would like to exhibit more self-control, prayerfully submit this area to God, and ask for guidance in dealing with it. Ask the Holy Spirit to provide you with the strength to change. Next, write down the area and list the reasons why you feel you have difficulties with it. These don't have to be particularly sophisticated. If overeating is a problem, for example, you might list such reasons as you simply enjoy eating and that you find yourself eating more during stressful times or during the holidays. Also list the circumstances that influence the behavior. You might find that you eat a lot of snacks toward the end of the day or when you watch television.

This list will provide you with an understanding of your problem and will help you come up with a plan of action. On another piece of paper, create such a plan. List ideas that will help you gain control in this area of your life. In the case of overeating, you might avoid walking by a particular store where you buy junk food, or take fruit to work with you and eat it late in the afternoon when you've determined that you are most prone to snack.

The next step is implementation. You should undertake this step with a sense of experimentation. If your plan doesn't work, then create another one and see if that one is more successful.

You should continue this experimentation even *after* you have achieved the desired change in your life. Relapses are common, and don't be surprised that after achieving a certain weight or a certain eating pattern, for example, that you begin to relapse after a period of time. If you *do* experience relapse, note the conditions under which it occurred and include this knowledge in your maintenance plan.

The above is a reasonable plan of change that follows from my own reading and understanding of psychology. It helps to add a spiritual dimension to your work in this area. This involves simply including God as a partner in whatever change you are undertaking. Keep a prayerful attitude as you plan for your change, and then experience God's presence in your daily activities as you implement your plan. It also helps to enlist the support of others, even if it is something as simple as telling them that you want to change. This creates a stronger sense of accountability. You can ask that they pray for you as you make your change. Such prayer is extremely powerful!

One other aspect about making changes involves instantaneous realizations or epiphanies. When you sense that you are out of control, or that you simply are not reacting to something in a way that you would like, you can make quick changes that don't require the planning process outlined above. For example, I noticed a couple of years ago that I was particularly cranky in the evenings after work, especially if it was late in the week. I tended to be short tempered with people if things didn't immediately go my way. After an incident in which I responded to a store clerk in a way that I was not particularly proud of, I determined that in the future I would refrain from shopping or running errands late in the week after work.

This had the immediate effect of preventing me from losing my temper or being unreasonable. It was a simple thing, but it has had big consequences as far as I am concerned. You may find that making a few such changes can have equally big consequences in your life. Be aware of where there is a lack of control in your life—and make quick changes to overcome it.

I will conclude this discussion by telling you not to become too obsessed with self-control: That is a *real* danger. Such an obsession has several negative consequences. You may become discouraged because of a perceived lack of success in your activities, which may cause you to blame God. Or you may go overboard and become *too* controlling. I suspect that too much control has something to do with such problems as anorexia, as well as intolerance of others. Self-obsession also gets in the way of a continued focus upon God. Realize that *total* self-control is beyond the reach for humans.

Self-control is a fruit of the Spirit and, as such, is something we can exhibit and enjoy as one of God's blessings. Take it seriously enough to *allow* God to help you to bring about needed changes. Be lighthearted enough about it to keep the desire for self-control from overwhelming you. Know what you can change and leave the rest to God.

Returning to Jim and Justin: Jim was able to stop his Friday evening drinking. He found that his relationship with Justin improved not just on Friday, but every day and night of the week, because they did not have to deal with the baggage of their weekly skirmish. While they do not have a perfect relationship, it is loving and one that I am sure will grow over the years. I'm certain that Justin will see Jim's greater degree of self-control as something he will be able to model with his own children when he becomes a father.

I will leave you with some verses by St. Paul in his letter to the Colossians. Although not specifically about self-control, these verses capture the wider context in which self-control takes place:

> Above all, clothe yourselves with love, which binds everything together in perfect harmony. And let the peace of Christ rule in your hearts, to which indeed you were called in the one body. And be thankful. Let the word of Christ dwell in you richly; teach and admonish one another in all wisdom; and with gratitude in your hearts sing psalms, hymns, and spiritual songs to God. And whatever you do, in word or deed, do everything in the name of the Lord Jesus, giving thanks to God the Father through him. (Col 3:14–17).

CHAPTER SIX
Mustard Seeds

*S*mall things sometimes yield big results. We often agonize over the big decisions, and ignore the fact that the small ones make up who we are and where we are going. Jesus' parables teach that the kingdom of heaven has this quality about it. In one parable it is like yeast that, once mixed with batter, becomes the key ingredient in making the bread rise (Matt 13:33). In another, the kingdom of heaven is like a mustard seed (Matt 13:31–32). It is the smallest of seeds when planted, but becomes huge as it matures.

There are many interpretations of these parables. One view I have is that the decision to become a Christian may only seem to be something a person does at a particular point in time. In a sense, just believing in something seems like a simple thing. Yet it has great consequences that continue as time progresses. Like yeast, it becomes a determining factor in a life. And like the mustard seed, spiritual growth is a very tangible result of such a decision.

A similar interpretation I would like to explore is that Christianity involves many other decisions that have large and tangible results. I am in good company in seeing the progress between our reactions to life's situations and spiritual growth. Saint Paul says in Romans that we should rejoice in our sufferings knowing that "suffering produces endurance, and endurance produces character, and character produces hope, and hope does not disappoint us, because God's love has been poured into our hearts through the Holy Spirit that has been given to us" (Rom 5:3–5).

The idea of character is worth exploring in detail. "Character is destiny," as the Greek philosopher, Heraclitus, wrote. Character is made up of the many small and large decisions that we make over the course of a day. It is truly an example of how *small* actions yield *big* results. A friend of mine, a company executive, is known for making wise decisions on difficult subjects. He is considered to be a man of great character. One thing I have noticed about him is that his character is not only displayed in the larger events of his day, but in the smaller ones as well. He is considerate to people he barely knows.

He takes the time to open doors for people carrying loads, and to stop and talk to people that others often pass by without so much as a thought. You can see the work of grace in what he does. All of his actions are indications of a person of great faith and character. In fact, I would say that if he stopped doing the small things, the large ones would suffer as well! That's what mustard seeds are all about.

Allowing the seed to grow in your life takes prayer and reflection upon God. I discussed in chapter three how to add such practices to your life. What I'd like to focus on here are the factors that may be getting in the way of mustard-seed growth and how you can overcome them. As far as small actions are concerned, it means not getting so caught up in your life that you fail to recognize that there are other people out there. Take the time to notice them and to care for them. Learn the names of the people that you pass by every day. Ask about their families and learn to be concerned about them. There are bound to be people that you can learn from, as well as those who need your help.

As far as larger concerns, find ways to mobilize yourself and others toward *service*. One obstructing factor is thinking that there is little that one individual can do to impact the world in a positive way. Added to this is the fact that most people don't work in jobs that are *directly* related to helping others. Such obstacles can be overcome, however. Currently, my part of the country is experiencing an increase in drug abuse, particularly crystal-meth. The area that I supervise conducts medical research related to health insurance benefits. On the surface, this has nothing to do with drug abuse. Yet I began to wonder if there is something that we can do to help address this situation in a positive way. Many of the people that work for me are experts in medical research, and one happens to have some skill in the field of drug abuse. I pulled the group together and asked if they would be willing to take this on as a project. I explained that since we can't ignore our tasks for our employer, this should take up no more than 5 percent of our time. The group eagerly took up this challenge and is currently contacting local authorities and experts to see how we can help. I believe that this effort will make a difference. This is my way of planting a mustard seed.

Another obstacle partially addressed by the approach above has to do with *time*. Most of us are busy people and really don't have much time on our hands. This, again, can be addressed by creating a project to work on during your existing schedule. If you work in finance, for example, see if some existing effort and expertise can be used to address the financial needs of the least advantaged. Think creatively to see what you can do.

Another approach is to engage in what I call "one-minute ministries." These are quick things that you can do that don't take much time out of your day. You might drop food off at a food bank on your way to work, for example, or take some clothing to a nearby shelter. Before your week starts, identify a few things that you can do and plan the time to do them. Remember and honor, too, the things that you are already doing. Caring for your children by helping them participate in sporting events, or visiting an elderly relative, is also consistent with mustard-seed thinking. Big things grow from small things. Writing, for me, is another mustard-seed activity. I may consider it as something I would do anyway, but I also like to think of it as an activity that I dedicate to God and to the service of others.

There is another activity consistent with mustard-seed growth that I recently came across. This one is from John Ortega's *If You Want to Walk on Water, You've Got to Get Out of the Boat*. Ortega encourages people to pick something and pray for it for six months. Something extraordinary will happen if you do this. He tells the true story of a man who decided to pray for Kenya for six months. He didn't know much about Kenya other than it was probably a place that could use some prayer. Within a short period of time he met a woman who had connections in Kenya and offered to take him there. While in Kenya he met the country's president and, walking around with him, saw some prisoners. He asked the president about them and was told that they were imprisoned for political reasons. He told the president that he should let them go.

When he returned to this country, he got a call from the U.S. State Department. They wanted to know what he had said to the president of Kenya, because he had released some prisoners that they had been trying to get released for years. The president asked the man to return to Kenya for three days to pray for him as he selected his new cabinet. This, indeed, is mustard-seed growth in action!

Within the Catholic Church there is even a program called Mustard Seed Communities that, along with the Paulist Press, sponsors a *Work the Word* program. This ministry uses a small group format to encourage reflection upon helping others and extending the word of God. It also contains a service mission outside of the United States as an important part of each group's activities. Program materials may be obtained through the Paulist Press, and information about this ministry can be found at www.mustardseed.com.

I encourage you to think of something for which you can pray for six months, or to join a ministry such as *Work the Word*. I believe that if you do one or both of these activities that you will indeed see extraordinary things take place.

Another activity that I would like for you to engage in is to ask yourself where you have seen mustard-seed growth in your life. Take a look at your past and present and see where you have experienced spiritual progress. This simple exercise yields a number of insights. For one, it enables you to see the mustard seed process firsthand. Many people tend to look at the negatives of their lives and where they feel that they may not be measuring up.

Changing your perspective can be an enormously positive experience. A man I know, John, undertook this task and remembered that when he was in his twenties he took on the work of leading a class on the

Bible at his church. Since he was trained in education, it was felt that he had specific skills that might help in this regard. He was not a biblical scholar by any stretch of the imagination, but was assisted by a good series of study books, such as Father Lawrence Boadt's *Reading the Old Testament*. He spent five years teaching the entire Bible. This helped him in a variety of ways. For one, he learned a great deal about the Bible both as a text and as a source of inspiration. He found that there was hardly an area of his life that did not improve as a result of this undertaking. Although he has since taken up other ministries and it has been nearly ten years since he finished teaching the Bible, he still remembers it fondly and finds that he is able to use the wisdom he gained from it in his interactions with others. What began as a relatively small undertaking blossomed into a great blessing.

Another benefit of thinking about spiritual growth is that it provides insight into your particular nature and God's will for you. We all have strengths and talents, and you can reflect on your areas of growth to get some idea of where you are likely to meet with personal successes. Returning once again to John, he discovered that his mustard-seed growth tended to be in areas such as teaching and communication. He is good at taking complex information and getting it across to others in ways that they can understand. As he thinks about where he can contribute and aid in extending the kingdom of heaven to others, he feels that it will be in those areas.

Taking stock of your life can be assisted by any number of personality inventories that can help you to determine where your personal abilities and growth areas may be. One that I like in particular is the Hartman Value Profile, which is based upon the work of philosopher Robert S. Hartman. The profile assesses an individual's value system and measures judgment in several key areas. It provides insight into where your strengths and weaknesses might be with respect to decision-making, and can even find areas where there may be imbalances between your personal and professional life.

Doctor C. Stephen Byrum, who is dean of the Spiritual Leadership Institute, has been using the Hartman Value Profile in helping organizations in their recruiting, retention, and decision-making efforts. One element that I particularly like about the survey, as explained to me by Dr. Byrum, is that it springs from Hartman's reaction to the evil of Nazi Germany. As a German who escaped Nazi Germany, Hartman saw firsthand how Adolph Hitler was masterful at organizing evil. Hartman spent his professional life thinking about goodness and how it can be effectively organized and accomplished. Further information about Robert S. Hartman, the Spiritual Leadership Institute, and the Hartman Value Profile may be found in the Annotated Bibliography.

This may sound like a bit of a philosophical discussion, but it is actually a practical one that fits well with mustard-seed thinking. While an instrument such as the Hartman survey is invaluable as far as understanding your moral and ethical decision-making strengths, you can already begin the process of working for good. Find people who are known to be superior as far as their ethical judgment is concerned. Read books that focus on ethics, such as Aristotle's *Nicomachean Ethics* or the more recent *Morality: An Introduction to Ethics (Canto)* by Bernard Williams. Then identify some shortcoming in society and start to think about how it can be addressed both immediately and systematically. If poverty is something you want to address, work with the poor while also thinking about the conditions that created the poverty. Come up with practical ways that get at the root of the problem. Start looking for places where you can plant seeds.

Before concluding this chapter, I would like to leave you with an idea that has been in the back of my mind for a long time. At some point I hope to write a book about it! I summarize it with the idea of doing good "on the side." Many people create sideline activities in their lives. Some people that have a hobby or another job outside of their normal line of work talk about doing it on the side.

You can make one of your sideline activities something that is consistent with mustard-seed thinking. Pick something that you feel called to do, and spend a little time each week doing it. Make it an experiment of sorts so that you can find activities that seem consistent with God's will for you. It doesn't necessarily have to be something consistent with charitable types of activities, although these are things you should take up from time to time. Try writing, painting, or making music in ways that you feel glorify God. Look for things that make you feel particularly energized and that also help others. Keep up your efforts, contemplating how you can better use them to extend God's kingdom.

Our role as Christians is to plant good seeds. There are likely dozens of ways you have seen the kingdom of heaven sprout in your own life. The main point of this chapter is to be *aware* of this process, and think about how you can foster it in the people and situations around you. This is one of the great gifts of Christian spirituality. Big things come from small actions. Small decisions make up who you are. Being kind to someone you have previously ignored or had conflict with, opening doors for strangers, and looking for ways that you can help others seem like small things—but the consequences can be tremendous.

CHAPTER SEVEN
Community

*T*ina often fantasizes about being a full-time composer and musician. She sees herself getting up at a reasonable hour, meditating, eating a light breakfast, and spending the rest of the day composing. In her fantasy she also doesn't have to deal much with other people. An introvert by nature, she finds that interacting with others takes something out of her. Her job as a school administrator has its rewards, but it often goes against the grain of her nature. She uses a variety of spiritual practices to make it through the day, but must still deal with the fact that she lives in a world that often values extroverts over introverts.

Although spiritual people come in all sizes, shapes, and colors, many, like Tina, have a solitary nature. This is not surprising since such spiritual activities as meditation and contemplation are often done alone. When we think of spiritual people we often think of those who struck out on their own to experience God or to find the truth. Monks and religious sisters also come to mind. Although they live in a community, solitude is a feature of many monastic orders. Hence, hermits live on the grounds of an abbey.

Still, even those who have struck out on their own or who have pursued the life of a contemplative monk or nun have to learn how to deal with others. Aristotle was right when he said that human beings are political or social animals. In many respects, we *need* one another to survive. We rely upon others for food and shelter, to say nothing of procreation and meeting our social needs. Studies on the importance of touch to infants indicate that the need for others is wired into our beings. From the beginning we need nurturing and support. But obtaining that support means that we have to interact with other people. And people are fickle at best!

Living in a community can be particularly difficult for the person with strong spiritual inclinations. Thomas Merton, the Trappist monk, is a good example of this. Merton joined a Trappist monastery in the early 1940s. His desire to get away from the world had something to do with it. But he also desired to live in a religious community. As he progressed in his vocation he longed for even *more* solitude. He sought to become a near total contemplative, and asked to be allowed either to live alone within his order or to join the Carthusians, which is an even more contemplative order.

Merton's desire for solitude, as well as his need for other people, was a constant source of tension in his life. This is evident in his writings as well as in the volumes of his journals that were published a few years ago. *The Intimate Merton: His Life from His Journals* and *A Thomas Merton Reader* are good books to read to become familiar with him (See these and other books by Thomas Merton listed in the Annotated Bibliography.). An ardent antiwar advocate during the early days of the Vietnam War (Merton died from an accidental electrocution in 1968.), Merton wanted to have an impact on the world. His correspondence with various people fills several volumes, indicating that he valued others and wanted to be in contact with them. Yet at the same time he also longed for solitude.

There are a number of ways those of us living in the world can deal with this tension. One is to try to honor the need for solitude while also finding a community of like-minded individuals who will help you deal with life. This can either be through joining some kind of formal group or through a loose community of friends. Either approach has its merits. Churches, of course, are an excellent source of community. A church provides a good alternative to our other communities. You may be able to find a sympathetic ear regarding the problems you face elsewhere. One thing to be aware of either in a church setting or any other type of group is that the people within them are not perfect, and even in church you will find others with whom you simply don't get along. The truth is that most of us have people in our lives that we seek to avoid. That just seems to be a part of humans and their societies.

Accepting this situation can go a long way toward being able to benefit from a community. Take a more detached view of the situation so that when you come across someone you don't like you are able to handle it more effectively. Don't give a lot of energy to the situation—unless, of course, you feel threatened in some way and need to find a solution. Otherwise, deal with the person straightforwardly but without making the situation more than it is—which might just be two people who don't get along.

Finding a community can be a little difficult for a solitary type. You need to be the one to take the first step, which may seem difficult. Still, it is usually a lot easier than it seems. All you have to do is show up! If you are already in a church but feel the need for another group to meet your needs, pick one that shares some interest, such as hiking, running, or reading. These are good places to practice spirituality, because *through* them you will be able to find people who are in need and who can also support you as you go through life. One other aspect that may be holding you back is a concern with getting overwhelmed with commitments. Attending church regularly typically means that eventually you'll be asked to do something for the church. You may have to teach a class, help with food preparation, or participate in some type of outreach effort. The same is true of being a member of just about any organization. Once you join, there will likely be some activities that you'll be asked to do.

Again, it's important to see both the possibilities and the pitfalls involved with such activities. You may find in teaching a class, for example, that you discover a hidden knack for leading that you didn't know about. You may also find that it isn't really what you are cut out to do, or that you simply don't have time to do the activity. Once again, I'll use Tina as an example. Tina has quite a few things going on in her life right now. The school where she works is implementing a new program that is both stressful and time-consuming. Her teenage son is a high school senior who is likely spending his last year at home. He also has a lot of sports activities that Tina likes to attend. The thought of adding anything *else* to her schedule is a bit much for her. Her best bet at present is to enjoy the community that she has with other parents and at church. She doesn't need to join any additional groups or find any *new* activities because she is already stretched too thin. In a year or two she will be in a different situation, but for now she doesn't need to seek out any new communities.

This brings up another aspect of communities. You can certainly draw on those in which you already live and work to gain spiritual support. Usually this involves taking a different perspective toward your day. Paying a little attention to people around you and being aware of their needs is one way of doing this. You can, in fact, see your existing community as a training ground for the practice of spirituality. When things seem to be taking a bad turn, or when you are not getting along with some important person in your life, use it as a means to grow spiritually. See if you can take a different view of what is going on around you. Also, see if you can find some means of dealing with the difficult person in a way that helps you grow. It's hard to advise you exactly how you should react to such a situation or to such a person. We all have our own unique growth areas. All situations, however, can help us get closer to God. *That* is the essence of spirituality.

I will tell you about a couple of failed attempts I have had with respect to community, because I am of the firm belief that failures teach us at least as much as successes. Like Tina, I tend to be a bit of a solitary type. I have also felt a need, at times, to be within a community. It may be because I moved around quite a bit growing up and didn't have the opportunity to benefit from long-lasting relationships. This left me with the desire to belong to something that is larger than myself. At one point, I attempted to create a community by getting together people whom I felt shared similar interests. This was a group that was involved with studying a particular aspect of culture from an intellectual standpoint. I scheduled some biweekly meetings and found a place for us to meet. Unfortunately, there were a couple of personalities in the group that just didn't mesh. As the meetings wore on, it became clear that this wasn't going to work out. I found myself feeling emotionally and spiritually drained after the meetings. No one complained when I stopped scheduling the meetings, which leads me to believe that they felt the same way.

Another negative example I have is from joining a well-established, nonprofit organization. Everything was fine until I came into conflict with an individual who was brought in from the outside to take a leadership role. Try as I might, I just couldn't get along with this person. In the end, I did everyone a favor by leaving. It was sad and difficult, but I felt that there simply wasn't another way of handling the situation. Sometimes you do have to leave.

In all of this it seems that our relationship with community is a dance of sorts. At times you will find people with shared interests with whom you interact well. At other times you will have difficulties within one or more of your communities. I remember a book from my days as a political science student called *Exit, Voice, and Loyalty*. Written by Albert O. Hirschman, the premise of the book is that people have three choices when they run into difficulties within an organization. They can leave, express their concerns and try to make changes, or be loyal and remain with the organization in spite of their disagreements. The same is true within the context of communities. When experiencing a disagreement with the community, we can decide to walk away, work for change, or remain loyal. A current example concerns the status of homosexuality within certain church denominations. Those that disagree with their churches' position on this issue, whatever that position may be, have the choice of leaving, expressing their disagreement, or deciding to remain loyal.

Community inevitably pushes us to make such decisions. Spirituality calls us to consider our actions prayerfully and from the perspective of loving God and loving one another. Whatever we decide within community should be with this, the greatest of commandments, in mind. We know that disagreements have been a part of the Christian church from the beginning. The issue of whether church members should live according to Jewish laws was intensely debated shortly after Jesus' death. The church eventually worked through this, but other issues and controversies rage on. In the end, it is best to see your relationship with your church as a means of experiencing God and loving others. Keep this in mind as you face whatever controversies lie ahead.

For all of the difficulties and imperfections contained within them, communities are where we are likely to experience our spiritual growth. This is where we will make our stands and our concessions. It is where we may be hurt or where we may hurt others. It is also where we will forgive and be forgiven.

Like Tina, many of us have fantasies about not having any responsibilities other than our own desire for creativity. We dream about not having to get up and go out into a world filled with difficult people and situations. Yet, like Tina, we have to face the fact that these are fantasies. We can still go out into the world with our good intentions and with the desire to be a source of inspiration to others. It is not easy to do this all of the time, but it is possible to do it some of the time. We also need to find the love and support that people in communities can provide.

With this, I feel that it is best to gravitate toward your friends and supporters, and to live in a spirit of forgiveness. Forgive past wrongs if you can. Be wise in doing this so that you don't get wronged again, but look for those situations where you may be bearing grudges that really aren't doing much besides creating conflict. As far as your friends are concerned, be open to them. Seek out other friends who are likely to provide you with the support you need.

Finally, be open to strangers and to the odd situations that are likely to present themselves. Since they are going to come along whether you want them to or not, welcome them with a warm heart and a loving spirit. Even if you never get to live your fantasy, learn to find the kingdom of heaven around you where you are and in what you do.

CHAPTER EIGHT
Holiness

*I*t is fitting that I am writing this during the week before Christmas—a time when holiness is never closer and yet, at the same time, never more distant. There are last minute shopping items to purchase and meals to plan amid the usual holiday chaos. Occasionally, we are reminded of what the real celebration is all about. As fleeting as these moments are, they can also be powerful reminders that the call to holiness is always with us.

Holiness can seem like a daunting task—so much so that some people never even consider it. But the call to the spiritual life is, in many respects, a call to holiness. A holy person is one whose life is characterized by a high degree of purity and reflects the ever-present love of God. Blessed Mother Teresa comes to mind, although there are less well-known people who also have these qualities.

The Christmas season is also a time when the year winds down and we begin to think about next year. While I don't make New Year's resolutions, I confess that I do think about the changes I would like to make and the goals I would like to achieve in the coming year. I often set goals for myself during the lull between Christmas and the New Year. Among these are ways that I'd like to progress spiritually.

Although spiritual transformation toward holiness may seem unattainable, it is an important way of looking at spiritual progress. Like most people, I don't see holiness as something that I will easily attain in my lifetime. I am too aware of my shortcomings and how difficult it would be to overcome them. I also know that, when it comes right down to it, my daily focus tends to be on *short-term* survival rather than *long-term* spiritual growth.

To be serious about spirituality, though, is to be serious about transformation and holiness. I link these two concepts because I see holiness as the goal of spiritual life and transformation as the processes by which we attain this goal. *Metanoia* is the classical Greek term that captures what I am saying. It means to undergo a deep spiritual conversion or change. Several disciplines have been developed and tried through the years to aid the process of *metanoia*. These include fasting, solitude, and prayer, to name just a few. On the extreme end, there have been people who lived on the tops of mountains, who deprived themselves of food and other creature comforts for long periods of time, and who wore hair shirts and practiced self-flagellation in order to be transformed. These aren't practices that I recommend.

It is hard to describe what holiness is exactly, though we all know people who exhibit holiness in their daily lives. It does involve ethical conduct, as well as a deep concern for others, although these don't capture all of it. There is a feeling that you get when you are around people who have something of the quality of holiness. To use a homonym, there is a sense of *wholeness* about them. Perhaps it is best to describe such people as exhibiting the qualities of *love* as captured by St. Paul in 1 Corinthians 13. That is, they are patient and kind rather than envious, boastful, arrogant, or rude. They aren't irritable or resentful and aren't happy about wrongdoing but rejoice in the truth. They believe, hope, and endure (see 1 Cor 13:4–7).

Throughout this book I have mentioned several spiritual practices that will help you as you go through your daily life. Are these enough to achieve holiness, or at least get a great deal closer to it? They might be, but there is another element that I'd like to include as well. This is the sense of openness to the Holy Spirit, a way of living that includes the notion of mystical direction. I once heard a speaker at a conference describe a particularly unique way of thinking about openness. She asked the group to think about the things that haunt them as individuals. That is, those thoughts or ideas that come into your mind that you can't seem to shake. It might be something that someone said, or perhaps a line from a song or a painting that, for some reason, is particularly meaningful. You can take these as invitations to which you can respond. Frequently, these are ideas that, if you took them seriously, would require you to make some changes in your life, or may require you to take up a new activity.

I'll give you an example of what I mean. Recently, I have been haunted by the idea of writing short stories. I have not written fiction for some time, but the plot lines of a couple of stories have come into my mind. As I am just now beginning to pursue this, I find that this is allowing me to explore a creative side of myself that has been dormant for some time. It deepens me as a person. Although I say this with all humility, I believe—or at least I *hope!*—that writing short stories will aid me in my progress toward holiness.

Obviously, this is something that is unique to me. I wouldn't say that people have to write short stories in order to progress spiritually. People will have other things that haunt them. It may be the idea of doing volunteer work in a health clinic or serving the homeless in a community kitchen. Like writing, it may be something only indirectly tied to serving God and others. Whatever it is, the haunting activity can be used as a spiritual exercise. I may write fiction that isn't spiritually based at all. Yet it will likely teach me to look at people in a particular way and learn to understand and appreciate them more. It may also lead to some self-healing, which will enable me to serve others a little better.

You may wonder what to do if you don't have anything that seems to be haunting you at the moment. This likely is just a matter of paying a little more attention to what you come across during the course of a day. You may hear someone say something that reaches you, or perhaps you may remember something you wanted to do when you were younger. You can also make a conscious effort to expose yourself to new people and surroundings to see if something comes of that. Try taking a different way to work or to the store, for example, or visit a museum or go to a play. Such activities are bound to bring about something that sticks in your mind.

People tend to think of God as communicating with them in some direct way. Yet I believe that there are numerous subtle, indirect ways that God speaks to us. It may be through a story that we hear or a new person that we come across. We can do more than simply say that the story is "interesting" or that the new person has a few ideas that we haven't heard before. We can use these instances as a means of living a more exciting and grace-filled life.

Another way to progress was an idea given to me by the CEO of a successful company; someone who served as my mentor for a year and gave me many valuable insights. One was that if I wanted to develop a particular skill, I should get myself put on a project that would force me to develop it. This is a good way of making yourself grow in ways that you would like to grow. I wanted to develop some entrepreneurial abilities, for example, so I managed to get put on a project that was a start-up business for the company where I worked. While the project was ultimately discontinued, I did learn a great deal about an area of business that I would not have learned otherwise.

From a spiritual perspective, you can identify some skill or trait that you would like to develop. You might want to learn how to be a more patient person, for example. You can then come up with ways that will force you to develop patience, such as putting yourself in situations where you have to deal with people who are somewhat difficult.

Obviously, this approach is *not* an easy one, and needs to be entered into with some caution. It is difficult to develop new skills. Chances are that if the skill came easily to you, you would have developed it by now. You will likely have to choose activities that are particularly difficult. The benefit of this approach is that it can create openness to God and others because it will make you grow in untapped areas. Such growth can always be put to the service of God.

There are a number of other ways that you can be open to God. You can pay attention to your dreams, for example, to see if there are messages there. Or you can wander through a bookstore to see if you are attracted to a particular title or a section of books. Some might see such approaches as a little too much aligned with New Age thinking and, indeed, you have to be careful about this. Still, we know that God occasionally does communicate to people through dreams, and does put things in people's lives as a means of pointing them in a certain direction.

It helps in whatever path of openness you choose to remain connected to people that you trust. You need others to be a reality check for you. If you stray down a path that is potentially damaging to yourself or to others, you need the help of trusted people to pull you back. The bottom line of any growth is whether it helps in loving God and other people. Don't get too confused in your thinking about this. If it helps, it helps—and if it doesn't, it doesn't. Don't pursue paths that may involve some short-term damage in the name of some long-term goal. Many times that approach just doesn't work.

In the end, holiness is a mystical process that can take a lifetime to achieve or can take place in a single moment. It took a long time for St. Augustine to find the path of holiness, while St. Paul was forced on the path while traveling to Damascus. It is hard to figure out why these things happen the way that they do. It is helpful, though, to pay attention to your spiritual progress toward holiness and continue to offer your life to God.

This is not an easy task in today's world. Doubts are everywhere, and it is hard to be a believing person in the face of deep intellectual skepticism as well as overzealous fundamentalism. It helps to connect to God as part of a daily pattern of life and to remember the difference it makes to be a believer. I saw the real difference that belief makes when I was looking for a job years ago. It was toward the end of my graduate school education, and I was calling on a loose network of people from my school that had graduated before me. The good thing was that since they had graduated and were already out in the world, many were well-connected. The bad thing was that since they started the program earlier than I did I really didn't know any of them very well. One of the other students told me to talk to an alumnus named Don, because he was a Christian and, therefore, likely to help. This wasn't because I was a Christian (I was), or that the person telling me was a Christian (he wasn't at the time), but because Don was just the kind of person who took his faith seriously and was more likely to help others.

I did give Don a call and found him to be extraordinarily caring and helpful. While I found a job through other means, Don's attitude and concern meant a lot to me. I never mentioned that I was a fairly new Christian at the time, or in any way indicated my faith. I didn't want to appear to be using that to gain his support. Don's willingness to listen and to help, though, was in stark contrast to some of the other people I called.

This to me is one aspect of what faith is all about. Any faith worth its salt ought to make a difference in the way you treat people. As far as Christians are concerned, our faith asks that we go the extra mile for all people, believers and nonbelievers alike. Although I haven't talked to Don in twenty years, his actions of the past continue to remind me of the difference that faith makes, and of the reality that faith creates. Skepticism and doubt are pushed aside by the simple fact that loving God and one another makes a visible difference.

Holiness seems more and more lost as I continue to go through this Christmas season. But maybe that is as much my fault as everyone else's. I haven't taken holiness seriously enough. I have allowed myself to become too focused on the commercial side of the holidays. For the world to change, *I* have to as well. In fact, I have to change *first*. I have to see and act with the knowledge and experience of the blessedness of this season. I have to take the call to holiness seriously and allow the Holy Spirit to be a transformative force in my life.

This is a good place to end this short consideration of various aspects of living a grace-filled life. Our faith can and should be an ongoing transformative process toward holiness. For me and for many others who feel the push and pull of the world, it isn't always easy. Each day I say my prayers and do my reading, and each day I emerge, *ready or not,* into a world that takes me in all kinds of directions. At the end of the day I am frequently worn out, and, as often as not, still have a few other tasks that I need to do. Sometimes problems or issues come out of nowhere, and I am forced to deal with things that I couldn't have anticipated. Luckily, these are interspersed with times of peace and grace.

Such is life. My hope is that somewhere along the way I can get better at living and can teach a little of what I've learned to others. What I know so far is that *faith makes a difference.* It may be hard to stay faithful in times as difficult as ours, but faith does matter. So, like St. Paul in 2 Timothy 4:7, we must fight the good fight. *Ready or not,* we must take our path to holiness seriously and use the results of our progress to feed a hungry world.

Afterword:
Ready or Not Reading

Grace has a way of reaching out to us in different ways and through various types of media. Even in a culture as seemingly secular as ours, we can experience the power of grace in movies, plays, music, paintings, sculptures, and writings. We can use these to sustain us as we go through life. I have often been amazed at how listening to a piece of music or studying a painting can open me to the experience of God's presence.

As I mentioned in chapter three, reading is one way to continue to grow in grace. Reading has always been important to me, and since this book somehow found its way into your hands (and you seem to have made it to the end), it is a safe bet that reading is important to you as well. I've often wondered after reading another author's book what reading plan I should undertake in order to continue to grow in the way that the book prescribed. With that idea in mind, I will leave you with the Annotated Bibliography that immediately follows. Since it is not, strictly speaking, a reading plan, I need to offer a few words of explanation about it.

Before I do that, however, I would like to provide a few thoughts about reading and spirituality in general. Since I think of spirituality as that which brings us closer to God, I think of *spiritual* reading as fostering that closeness. Of course, not all reading does that. I have to read a lot of technical material as part of my job, and although I often find it interesting, it doesn't particularly move me to experience anything other than an increase in knowledge. That's not to say that it can't motivate me in spiritual ways, and I need to look for that to happen from time to time. Occasionally, I will read something at work that enables me to experience God or that provides me with the information I need to help someone else (and allows me to experience God in that way). But this is not a frequent occurrence.

Since that experience doesn't often happen with my professional reading, and since reading itself is important to me, I consciously set aside times for spiritual reading and reflection. Reading in these instances connects me with the thoughts and wisdom of people who are concerned, as I am, with experiencing grace and growing in the knowledge of God. This may be through an insight that I haven't had in the past or a deepening of a current understanding. Because it is such an intensely personal experience, reading also helps me to understand something of myself—what I as a person am attracted to, repulsed by, or willing to commit to intellectually. This is especially true of spiritual reading, since spirituality, like reading, has a personal dimension to it.

My points, then, are that reading is a powerful avenue of spiritual growth and can be an important part of your experience of God. It is deeply personal and, like anything involving grace, contains many insights and exciting surprises along the way. Saint Paul encourages us in Romans 12:12 not to be conformed to the pattern of this world. Since there are so many negative and *ungraceful* patterns in the world, it is necessary to take conscious action to expose yourself to positive and *graceful* ones. Reading has a way of doing that—of enabling you to be conformed not to the pattern of the flesh but to that of the Spirit. And, as I said, this process can be meaningful and exciting.

Allow me to offer a few personal examples of this experience. I was first exposed to the writings of Thomas Merton when I was in high school. There was something fascinating about this man who had literary ambitions and earthly desires, yet put these aside in order to join a monastery. Although I could sense that I didn't have a monastic vocation in my future, there was something about Merton the man and the writer that fascinated me. I have dipped into his work occasionally and have always come away with new insights. Initially they had to do with being open, as Merton was, to other religious traditions and learning from them. Then it was a deeper appreciation for meditation and contemplation. Most recently, it has been an appreciation for the various struggles we all have over our past decisions, struggles that Merton knew all too well. Reading Merton has provided me with a rich array of insights and observations. He managed to express things that I have felt but have been unable to put into words.

It's been almost ten years since I first read Brother Lawrence's *The Practice of the Presence of God and the Spiritual Maxims*. This small book had an equally profound influence upon my life. I had never thought about God as an ongoing experience, or that I could include God in my daily activities. At the time I came across this book, I was deeply in need of that message. It enabled me to think of God as capable of being experienced in daily life and not just during times of contemplation or during religious services. The book reached me with a message that was vital to me at that particular time and place. I return to Brother Lawrence occasionally to remind myself of his message.

Reading can do the same for you if it hasn't already. The following Annotated Bibliography offers several jumping-off points for you. Rather than come up with a plan of reading for you, I encourage you to create one of your own. I offer one or two descriptive sentences beneath each title as a way of helping you. It may be that you want to start with Benedictine spirituality and progress to healing and prayer. Or, you may want to start with older texts, such as *The Imitation of Christ*, and stay there for a while. Go where the Spirit leads you.

As you read, I encourage you to use a journal or some other written format to record your thoughts. This helps you to reflect more succinctly upon what you've read, and to remember it as well. You don't need to make this particularly complicated or difficult. Just write down the most important points from the book and go back to these occasionally to refresh your memory—as well as your soul! I also encourage you to return to the Bible from time to time no matter what reading plan you undertake. For me, it is the bedrock of faith, and my spiritual reading tends to deepen my reading of the Bible, just as the Bible deepens my spiritual reading. I return to the Bible often and am richly rewarded every time.

One other thing before you turn to the Annotated Bibliography. You will see that I've included some Internet Web sites as well. The Internet is a great source of both general and specific information, and you can certainly find reading material there to help you grow. It can also provide you with up-to-date information regarding support groups, spiritual communities, and the like. Since a complete listing of Internet sites would run for several pages and would be out-of-date the minute it is published, I have only listed a few representative sites.

Although the list of books is considerably longer, it, too, is only a representative list. A comprehensive list on centering prayer, for example, would run for several pages. Take this as a starting point, and realize that for every book on the list, there are many more that could just have easily been mentioned.

Use this Annotated Bibliography to open your heart and mind to whatever God has in store for you. Allow the reading contained herein to be a source of inspiration to transformation in your life. Finally, be willing to share the results of your reading with others so that they, too, can grow.

Annotated Bibliography

Books

Albom, Mitch. *The Five People You Meet in Heaven*. New York: Hyperion, 2003.

    A short book that is really more of a meditation on the meaning of life than a work of fiction. It provides insights into how our lives are intertwined and why this is important from a spiritual standpoint.

Aristotle. *The Nicomachean Ethics*. Translated by J. A. K. Thomson, edited by Hugh Tredennick. London: Penguin Classics, 2004.

    A true classic and a good place to begin a study of ethics, morality, and the good life.

Boadt, Lawrence. *Reading the Old Testament: An Introduction*. Mahwah, NJ: Paulist Press, 1985.

A thorough introduction to the Old Testament that sets it within the times and traditions in which it was written. A good commentary such as this is invaluable to an understanding of the Old Testament.

Byrum, C. Stephen and Leland Kaiser. *Spirit for Greatness: Spiritual Dimensions of Organizations and their Leadership*. Littleton, MA: Tapestry Press, Ltd., 2004.

One of the few books that really digs down into the depths of what it means to be an ethical and spiritually concerned leader in today's society. It is especially helpful to those who want to create good organizations.

Chittister, Joan. *In Search of Belief*. Liguori, MO: Liguori/Triumph, 2006.

Written by a Benedictine nun, this book presents personal meditations on the Nicene Creed. While her opinions will not be palatable to all, her method of reading, reflection, and writing is worth considering as a discipline.

————. *Wisdom Distilled from the Daily: Living the Rule of St. Benedict Today*. San Francisco: HarperSanFrancisco, 1990.

Chittister explains how Benedictine spirituality can be carried over into daily living. She demonstrates how commonplace things and occurrences can possess deep meaning.

Chodron, Pema. *When Things Fall Apart: Heart Advice for Difficult Times*. Boston: Shambhala, 2000.

It can be illuminating to read books from other traditions to see how they deal with life's difficulties. Chodron is a Buddhist who has written many books that are worth considering for their ability to help people to use life's difficulties as a means of developing compassion.

De Caussade, Jean-Pierre. *The Sacrament of the Present Moment*. San Francisco: HarperSanFrancisco, 1989.

A Jesuit priest from the eighteenth-century writes about how to experience each moment as a sacrament. Among other things, this can result in a joyous and more frequent experience of God's love.

Dyer, Wayne W. *The Power of Intention*. Carlsbad, CA: Hay House, 2004.

This is a good example of the many books that Wayne Dyer has written in the "power of positive thinking" vein. The books are helpful in fostering a positive outlook, but may give the impression that people have total control over the situations they face.

Fletcher, Anne M. *Sober for Good: New Solutions for Drinking Problems—Advice from those Who have Succeeded*. New York: Houghton Mifflin, 2002.

Alcohol abuse is hard for anyone to face. Fletcher sought out "masters" who succeeded in dealing with their abuse and offers strategies based upon their advice. This is a practical book that comes straight from the mouths of those who have been successful in dealing with their addictions.

Foster, Richard J. *Seeking the Kingdom: Devotions for the Daily Journey of Faith*. San Francisco: HarperSan-Francisco, 1995.

A sound thirty-day plan for transformative Christian living. It is helpful to use books of this sort to achieve spiritual growth during a set period of time.

―――. *Celebration of Discipline: The Path to Spiritual Growth*. San Francisco: HarperSanFrancisco, 1998.

A popular book that outlines various practices as tools for spiritual progress.

Hartman, Robert. *Freedom to Live: The Robert Hartman Story (Value Inquiry Book, Vol. 7)*, edited by Arthur R. Ellis. Kenilworth, NJ: Editions Rodopi, 1994.

Hartman's life and thoughts are in many ways reactions to his firsthand experience of the moral degradation of Hitler's Germany. His approach to ethics and the importance of creating a system of good are worth considering.

Hirschman, Albert O. *Exit, Voice, and Loyalty: Responses to Decline in Firms, Organizations, and States*. Cambridge, MA: Harvard University Press, 2004.

A now classic analysis of the choices people have when faced with various organizational and political difficulties. This is an example of how ideas from other disciplines, such as political science, can be helpful to religious and spiritual understanding and action.

Jones, L. Gregory. *Embodying Forgiveness: A Theological Analysis.* Grand Rapids, MI: Wm. B. Eerdmans Publishing Company, 1995.

An insightful and thought-provoking book that ventures beyond forgiveness into such areas as how to expand the kingdom of heaven through practicing the various "crafts" of Christian virtue.

Keating, Thomas. *The Kingdom of God Is Like....* New York: Crossroad Classic, 1997.

A fresh look at the parables from one of the foremost writers on Christian contemplation and centering prayer.

Kelty, Matthew. *Sermons in a Monastery: Chapter Talks,* edited by William O. Paulsell. Kalamazoo, MI: Cistercian Publications, 1983.

A little-known but inspirational book from a contemporary monk. I particularly enjoyed his story of a stray dog that was taken in by his monastery. We need to be open to the strangers, both furry and human, that find their way into our lives.

Kempis, Thomas à. *The Imitation of Christ.* Notre Dame, IN: Ave Maria Press, 1989.

Imitating Christ is one of the most important ways to grow spiritually. Written in the fifteenth-century, this book contains many practical ideas and suggestions for undertaking this discipline. It is also one of the most popular spiritual books of all time.

Lawrence, Brother. *The Practice of the Presence of God and the Spiritual Maxims*. Mineola, NY: Dover Publications, 2005.
        A life-changing book that shows how to include God in your daily activities.

MacNutt, Francis. *Healing*. Notre Dame, IN: Ave Maria Press, 1999.
        An influential study that answers such important questions as why prayer doesn't always lead to physical healing.

Marett-Crosby, Anthony. *The Benedictine Handbook*. Collegeville, MN: Liturgical Press, 2003.
        A book that includes important essays by leading thinkers in Benedictine spirituality. It also includes the *Rule of St. Benedict* in its entiery.

Mathis, Rick. *Making More of Life with Less: Seeking Humility, Simplicity, and Silence*. Liguori, MO: Liguori/ Triumph, 2004.
        My study of the monastic virtues of humility, simplicity, and silence.

———. *Prayer-Centered Healing: Finding the God Who Heals*. Liguori, MO: Liguori Publications, 2000.
        A look at the importance of prayer to healing.

————. *The Christ-Centered Heart: Peaceful Living in Difficult Times*. Liguori, MO: Liguori/Triumph, 1999.

A look at how to live with Christ at the center.

Meehan, Bridget. *The Healing Power of Prayer*. Liguori, MO: Liguori Publications, 1995.

A small book that shows how prayer can be applied to various physical, emotional, and spiritual ailments.

Merton, Thomas. *The Inner Experience*, edited by William H. Shannon. San Francisco: HarperSanFrancisco, 2003.

A posthumously published book by the famous Trappist monk that contains many excellent insights into spiritual and contemplative living.

————. *The Intimate Merton: His Life from His Journals*, edited by Patrick Hart and Jonathan Montaldo. San Francisco: HarperSanFrancisco, 1999.

A condensed version of Merton's multivolume journals. It is inspirational in showing that even those with profound spiritual insight struggle with the difficulties of life.

————. *The Asian Journal of Thomas Merton*, edited by Naomi Burton Stone, Patrick Hart, and James Laughlin. Consulting editor Amiya Chakravarty. New York: New Directions Publishing Corp., 1975.

Includes what in my opinion are among the best of Merton's journal writings. He wrote of his direct experiences with the religious traditions of Asia and how these deepened his understanding of God.

—————. *A Thomas Merton Reader,* edited by Thomas P. McDonnell. New York: Image, 1974.
Selections from Merton's essays, books, and poems. This is a good place to start a study of this prolific author.

—————. *Contemplation in a World of Action.* Garden City, NY: Doubleday, 1971.
The title itself sums up a difficulty that many spiritually inclined people have. As always, Merton's insights are helpful.

—————. *The Seven Story Mountain.* San Diego: Harcourt Brace Jovanovich, 1948.
Merton's first book chronicles his spiritual journey from secular living to his first years at the Abbey of Gethsemane in Kentucky. One of the best spiritual autobiographies of the modern age.

Morris, Debbie and Gregg Lewis. *Forgiving the Dead Man Walking.* Grand Rapids, MI: Zondervan, 1998.
Tells the story behind the movie *Dead Man Walking* from the perspective of one of the victims. A harrowing account of how a woman came to find faith and forgiveness in the face of evil.

Mott, Michael. *The Seven Mountains of Thomas Merton.* Boston: Houghton Mifflin, 1984.

An excellent and exhaustive biography of Thomas Merton. Mott captures the various stages of Merton's life and his complex spiritual journey.

Mulholland, M. Robert, Jr. *The Deeper Journey*. Downers Grove, IL: InterVarsityPress, 2006.
A discussion of how to overcome your "false self" in order to become closer to God.

Norris, Kathleen. *The Cloister Walk*. New York: Riverhead Books, 1996.
Written by an oblate, or lay associate of a monastery, this best-seller created a renewed interest in Benedictine spirituality. It is notable for its honesty in dealing with both the peaks and valleys of life.

Ortberg, John. *God Is Closer than You Think: If God Is always with Us, Why Is He so Hard to Find?* Grand Rapids, MI: Zondervan, 2005.
A modern look at spiritual living that draws inspiration from Brother Lawrence's *Practice of the Presence of God and the Spiritual Maxims*.

—————. *If You Want to Walk on Water, You've Got to Get Out of the Boat*. Grand Rapids, MI: Zondervan, 2001.
A great resource for creating change in your life. This book is a forceful push to those who find themselves stuck in dull and unexciting lives.

Palmer, Parker. *A Hidden Wholeness: The Journey toward an Undivided Life*. San Francisco: Jossey-Bass, 2004.

A Quaker with a doctorate in sociology, Palmer addresses the importance of community to spiritual living.

————. *Let Your Life Speak: Listening for the Voice of Vocation.* San Francisco: Jossey-Bass, 2000.
Palmer uses himself as an example of how looking over your life story can reveal deep truths about your nature. He candidly discusses his bout with depression and how he has dealt with various career decisions.

Peck, M. Scott. *The Road Less Traveled: A New Psychology of Love, Traditional Values and Spiritual Growth.* New York: Touchstone, 1998.
A popular book that spent months on the bestseller list in the late 1970s. This book reflects the modern interest in spirituality and spiritual growth.

Pennington, M. Basil. Lectio Divina: *Renewing the Ancient Practice of Praying the Scriptures.* New York: Crossroad Publishing Company, 1998.
A short guide to an important spiritual practice. *Lectio Divina* involves a slow and meditative reading of the scriptures. Pennington does a good job of explaining this practice.

————. *Centering Prayer: Renewing an Ancient Christian Prayer Form.* New York: Image, 1982.
Pennington ranks with Thomas Keating in importance as an advocate of centering prayer. This is an excellent introduction to the discipline.

Price, Reynolds. *A Whole New Life: An Illness and a Healing.* New York: Plume, 1995.

 Southern writer Reynolds Price describes his ordeal with cancer and his surprising experiences with prayer.

Rubin, Charles. *Don't Let Your Kids Kill You: A Guide for Parents of Drug and Alcohol Addicted Children.* Sonoma County, CA: NewCentury Publishers, 2004.

 Facing the addiction of a family member can be one of the greatest difficulties of life. This book gives useful advice to those in such situations.

Sanford, Agnes. *Healing Light.* New York: Ballantine Books, 1983.

 A classic book on the power of prayer and healing from one of its most successful practitioners.

Seligman, Martin. *Authentic Happiness: Using the New Positive Psychology to Realize Your Potential for Lasting Fulfillment.* New York: Free Press, 2002.

 A scientifically based look at what fosters happiness. In my view, happiness is related to the sense of joy that the spiritually inclined often experience.

Shinn, Florence Scovel. *The Writings of Florence Scovel Shinn.* Camarillo, CA: DeVorss & Company, 1988.

 In some ways a precursor to Wayne Dyer, but from a decidedly more Christian perspective. Her writings share many of the same strengths and weaknesses as those of Dr. Dyer.

Steindl-Rast, David. *Gratefulness, the Heart of Prayer: An Approach to Life in Fullness*. Ramsey, NJ: Paulist Press, 1984.

A powerful book on methods for including gratefulness in your life from a member of the Camaldolese order of monks.

Swinburne, Richard. *The Existence of God*. New York: Oxford University Press, 2004.

A challenging book that relies upon principles of logic to argue for the probability of the existence of God.

―――. *The Resurrection of God Incarnate*. New York: Oxford University Press, 2003.

An application of logic that argues not only for the existence of God, but also for a God that is consistent with the life and ministry of Jesus and the theology of Christianity.

Willard, Dallas. *The Divine Conspiracy : Rediscovering Our Hidden Life in God*. San Francisco: HarperSanFrancisco, 1998.

A philosopher's look at how to imitate Christ in today's world. This book is particularly helpful in offering clear and practical thinking about how to be a disciple of Christ.

Williams, Bernard. *Morality: An Introduction to Ethics (Canto)*. Cambridge: Cambridge University Press, 1993.

An introductory text that puts complex ethical ideas in understandable terms. This is a good place to achieve a basic understanding of the various schools of modern ethical thought.

Wiseman, Richard. *The Luck Factor: Changing Your Luck, Changing Your Life—the Four Essential Principles.* New York: Miramax Books, 2003.

One of the few books that looks at how seemingly "lucky" people actually create their luck through the way they react positively to life's situations. This is an example of how a positive (and, I would argue, grace-filled) outlook can, indeed, be life changing.

Web sites

"Alcoholics Anonymous." Available from http://www.alcoholics-anonymous.org.

Site of the most widely known approach to dealing with alcoholism and recovery.

"The Christian Classics Ethereal Library." Available from http://www.ccel.org.

A wonderful source for electronic books from all eras of Christian history. Contains a section of writings from the early church fathers.

"Contemplative Outreach, Ltd.—Resources and Programs for Centering Prayer." Available from http://www.centeringprayer.com.

Contains programs related to centering prayer and contemplation.

"Guest House." Available from http://www.guesthouse.org.

A treatment program for Catholic priests, deacons, brothers, or sisters suffering from an addiction.

"Mustard Seed Communities." Available from http://www.mustardseed.com.

A community specifically dedicated to furthering God's kingdom by working with the poor.

"Narcotics Anonymous, NA." Available from http://www.na.org/.

This organization truly changes the lives of those suffering from addiction.

"The Order of Saint Benedict (OSB)." http://www.osb.org.

A comprehensive site with many resources for those interested in monasticism and monastic communities.

"Q2HR—Home of the Hartman Value Profile." https://www.q2hr.com/.

Contains information on the Hartman Value Profile with specific applications to hiring employees.

"Robert S. Hartman Institute for Formal and Applied Axiology." http://www.hartmaninstitute.org/frames.html.

Dedicated to the work of Hartman and the study of axiology or value and value theory. Contains books, a membership directory, and a newsletter.

"Society for the Study of Christian Spirituality." Available from http://sscs.press.jhu.edu.

Studies a wide range of spiritual issues from a scholarly perspective.

"The Spiritual Leadership Institute: Spirituality in Business." Available from http://www.spirit4greatness. com.
Ideas and resources for applying spirituality to leadership and business.

"Thomas Merton Center." Available from http://www. merton.org.
Focuses on the life and work of Thomas Merton.

The Prayer of St. Francis

Lord, make me an instrument of Thy peace;
where there is hatred, let me sow love;
where there is injury, pardon;
where there is doubt, faith;
where there is despair, hope;
where there is darkness, light;
and where there is sadness, joy.

O Divine Master,
grant that I may not so much seek to be consoled
    as to console;
to be understood, as to understand;
to be loved, as to love.
For it is in giving that we receive,
it is in pardoning that we are pardoned,
and it is in dying that we are born to Eternal Life.

Amen.

ILLUMINATIONBOOKS

Other Books in the Series

Healing Mysteries
    by Adrian Gibbons Koester

Carrying the Cross with Christ
    by Joseph T. Sullivan

Saintly Deacons
    by Deacon Owen F. Cumming

Finding God Today
    by E. Springs Steele

Hail Mary and Rhythmic Breathing
    by Richard Galentino

The Eucharist
    by Joseph M. Champlin

Gently Grieving
    by Constance M. Mucha

Devotions for Caregivers
    by Marilyn Driscoll

Be a Blessing
    by Elizabeth M. Nagel

The Art of Affirmation
    by Robert Furey

Jesus' Love Stories
    by John F. Loya & Joseph A. Loya

Compassionate Awareness
    by Adolfo Quezada